IRAN

MIDDLE EAST
REGION IN TRANSITION
IRAN

Edited by Laura Etheredge, Associate Editor, Middle East Geography

Britannica Educational Publishing
in association with
ROSEN
EDUCATIONAL SERVICES

Published in 2011 by Britannica Educational Publishing
(a trademark of Encyclopædia Britannica, Inc.)
in association with Rosen Educational Services, LLC
29 East 21st Street, New York, NY 10010.

Distributed exclusively by Rosen Educational Services.
For a listing of additional Britannica Educational Publishing titles, call toll free (800) 237-9932.

First Edition

Library of Congress Cataloging-in-Publication Data

Iran / edited by Laura S. Etheredge.—1st ed.
p. cm.—(Middle East: region in transition)
"In association with Britannica Educational Publishing, Rosen Educational Services."
Includes bibliographical references and index.
ISBN 978-1-61530-308-3 (library binding)
1. Iran. 2. Iran—History. I. Etheredge, Laura.
DS254.5.I7314 2011
955—dc22

2010018317

Manufactured in the United States of America

On the cover (clockwise from top left): The ancient city of Yazd; Urban sociologist Masserat Amir Ebrahimi in a Tehrān coffee shop; Iranian leader Ayatollah Ali Khamenei casts his vote during the country's 2009 presidential election; Muslims gathered to pray at Imam Mosque in Eṣfahān, Iran. © *www.istockphoto.com/javarman3; Kaveh Kazemi/Hulton Archive/Getty Images; Olivier Laban-Mattei/AFP/Getty Images; Shutterstock.com*

On pages 1, 14, 28, 47, 59, 77, 162, 164, 167: An illustration depicting a polo match from the *Shāh-nāmeh*, a national epic by the Persian poet Ferdowsī. *Hulton Archive/Getty Images*

CONTENTS

44

57

71

93

106

127

134

143

INTRODUCTION

Framed by headlines and newsreel, events in Iran have long captivated the West. Yet current events have also led to troubled relationships between Iran and some of its neighbours in the international community—in particular the United States, which broke diplomatic relations with Iran in the 1980s. Today, the status of Iran's political freedoms, human rights, and nuclear proliferation are among the topics most familiar to Westerners discussing Iran, and in some cases, these topics have been responsible for colouring perceptions of Iran as a whole. Although such issues are indeed of great importance, a failure to identify them in the context of the broader realities of Iranian history and culture is to obscure the complex and diverse traditions of a land whose history spans millennia. In this volume, you will be introduced to the vivid and varied texture of Iran's social, political, geographic, and historical fabric.

Iran's physical properties are marked by sharp contrast. The country is dominated by a forbidding desert centre ringed by mountains, while to the north and south, relatively narrow coastal regions lie beyond. Tehrān, the capital, is seated at the foot of Mount Damāvand, the highest peak in the Elburz Mountain range and the country's highest point. Iran bears a number of volcanic regions, and earthquakes are both frequent and destructive. In the 20th century, 12 earthquakes measuring at least 7.0 on the Richter scale killed many thousands of citizens.

In addition to smaller streams, three major rivers drain the country; although only one is navigable, other waterways provide sources for irrigation and hydroelectric power. In the far northwest of the country, Lake Urmia—the country's largest inland body of water—spans

An illustration from the Shāh-nāmeh *("Book of Kings"), by Persian poet Ferdowsī.* The Bridgeman Art Library/Getty Images

some 2,000 square miles (3,119 square km). Iran's climate can range from subtropical to subpolar, and differences in elevation and proximity to the seacoast, mountains, or desert greatly affect regional temperature and precipitation. In northern and western Iran, there are four distinct seasons, while in the south and east, autumn and spring are effectively absorbed into a mild winter and a hot summer.

Physical and climactic variations influence the flora and fauna in various parts of the country. The Caspian region is well forested, and deciduous trees such as elm, beech, and linden, as well as fauna such as cheetahs and pheasants, are found there. In the mountains, which are also wooded, gazelles, leopards, and bears roam. Almond and wild fruit trees grow in the dry plateau, while desert dunes are capable of retaining enough water to support brush thickets. A remarkable diversity of amphibian life has been found in the southeast, southwest, and along the slopes of the Elburz and Zagros ranges, while the Persian Gulf is inhabited by some 200 species of fish. Although the Caspian Sea has far fewer species, it can lay claim to a fish of particular economic value: sturgeon, the source of the roe from which caviar is produced.

Iran is culturally diverse, although people of Persian ancestry predominate. Important Turkic, Arab, and Kurdish elements are also present, and there are numerous smaller ethnic groups. Persian (Farsi) is the official language of Iran, and some form of it is spoken by more than half the population. Azerbaijanian, Kurdish, Armenian, Lurī, and other languages are also found, although they are less widely spoken. Arabic is also spoken by a small proportion of the population, but, as the language of the Qur'ān, it has profound significance from a historical and religious standpoint. Over time, many Arabic words have been incorporated into the Persian language, and Arabic terms make up some one-third of the Persian lexicon.

Most of the population is Shīʿite Muslim, and Twelver Shīʿism is the official state religion. Twelver Shīʿites await the return of the 12th imam, Muḥammad al-Mahdī al-Ḥujjah, a messianic figure who is believed to have been concealed by God since his disappearance in the 9th century and who will return at the last judgement. The absence of the imam led indirectly to the rise of the Shīʿite clergy that continue to dominate Iran. Since there is no concept of ordination in Islam, the role of the clergy is filled by the ulama, a community of scholars whose members are Muslim men who have at least studied in a madrasah. Religious minorities in Iran include Sunni Muslims, Bahāʾīs, Christians, and Zoroastrians.

Isolation from the international community has been a significant obstacle to Iranian economic development, and embargoes on Iranian oil and bans on investment have also been detrimental. Rates of inflation and unemployment are high, and in a country where a large proportion of the population is young, urban, and literate, governmental failure to create adequate opportunities has frustrated many young, educated Iranians in recent years.

Iran's form of governance is a combination of Islamic theocracy and parliamentary democracy, overseen by the ulama. This blended form of government is rationalized in the concept of the *velāyat-e faqīh* ("governance of the jurist"), put forth by Ayatollah Ruhollah Khomeini. This concept provides that, in the absence of the divinely inspired imam, a qualified jurist is to be invested with political leadership. Extensive authority is thus wielded by the leader, or *rahbar*, a ranking cleric selected by the Assembly of Experts. Iran's president, who is responsible for the everyday operations of the government, is popularly elected to a four-year term, although candidates must be pre-approved. The Majles is Iran's unicameral legislative body, while the judicial system—which consists of a Supreme Court, a Supreme Judicial Council, and lower courts—functions on the basis of traditional Islamic principles.

Iran's cultural heritage is extensive, and cultural production in Iran is diverse. Iran is renowned for the quality of its carpets, the design of which varies by region. Textiles, pottery, and many wood, metal, and stone goods are also produced. Visual arts are at odds with the Islamic taboo on idolatry, but before the 19th century, miniature painting was a thriving art form in Iran. Classical literary works, such as those by Ferdowsī, Ḥāfeẓ, and Rūmī, are part of the rich tradition of Persian literature, but distribution of classical works has been difficult under the Islamic regime. Since the Islamic revolution, a great deal of modern Iranian literature has been produced by authors in exile.

Although the region had long been influenced by foreign and local dynasties, with the arrival of Islam in the 7th century, the social fabric of Iran was forever changed. The Arabs' decisive defeat of the Sāsānids in 636/637 marked not only an end, but a new beginning: Within two centuries, Persian culture was revived in an amalgamated form that acknowledged both its pre-Islamic heritage and contributions delivered by the Arab conquest.

Local opposition to the Damascus-based Umayyad dynasty was harnessed in a revolution led by Abū Muslim beginning in 747. With the fall of the Umayyads shortly thereafter, power passed to the 'Abbāsid dynasty, which, basing itself in Baghdad, reoriented the caliphate eastward. The 'Abbāsids considered themselves to be more pacific than the Umayyads, but rebellion within the empire had to be dealt with. In a period known as the Iranian Intermezzo (821–1055), independent groups such as the Ṣaffārids, Sāmānids, and Būyids exerted their autonomy at the expense of the 'Abbāsids.

The invasion of the Turkic Seljuqs, led by Ṭoghrıl Beg, marked the end of the Iranian Intermezzo. After capturing Baghdad in 1055, the Seljuqs worked to expand their empire, the broadening and maintenance of which required a large and expensive army. Soldiers were compensated with land grants, which formed the basis of petty principalities that increased in scope as central power weakened. The last Seljuq sultan was captured in 1153, and subsequent strife in the early 13th century was significant enough to upset trade through the area. This attracted the attention of Mongol leader Genghis Khan, who, having taken Beijing in 1215, had cause to be concerned about the interruption of trade from China. When trade and diplomatic missions were met with massacre, Genghis Khan turned to warfare. In 1220–21 the Mongols dealt the region a powerful blow and eventually gained control of portions of Iran, while other areas fell into disorder. In 1258 Genghis Khan's grandson Hülegü Khan assailed Baghdad, overthrowing the last 'Abbāsid caliph. Iran was made a base for further expansion, but the Mamlūks of Egypt prevented Hülegü and his successors from realizing this goal by defeating the Mongol army at 'Ayn Jālūt in 1260. Instead, a dynasty of Mongol deputy khans ("Il-Khans"), subservient to the great khan in China, was established.

Power was subsequently held by the Timurids (the descendents of the conqueror Timur, who had entered Iran in 1380) and the Kara Koyunlu and Ak Koyunlu Turkmen confederations before the Shīʿite Ṣafavids succeeded in supplanting the Ak Koyunlu in 1501. The strength of the Ṣafavids—who had captured much of Iran—rested in part on the successful conversion of the Turkmen tribes that became the core of their military effort. In the mid-17th century the central authority of the Ṣafavids was waning, however, opening a channel for the rise of the Shīʿite clergy in judicial and administrative concerns. Under the Qājār dynasty, which came to power at the end of the 18th century, European influence grew markedly as a diplomatic rivalry between Russia and Britain was touched off at Iran's expense.

Under Nāṣer al-Dīn Shah (1848–96), funds raised by granting concessions to foreign companies over resources and commodities were squandered, to the dismay of both the ulama and the mercantile class. Popular protest later sparked the Constitutional Revolution in 1905–6, which forced the granting of a constitution and led to the opening of the first Majles in late 1906. Under Russian pressure, the Majles was dissolved in 1911, however, and until the start of World War I, Iran was essentially governed by Russia. Following World War I, first the Russians and then, reluctantly, the British withdrew from Iran.

In 1925 an Iranian officer named Reza Khan seized power and had himself crowned Reza Shah Pahlavi. As shah, he pursued selective reforms while suppressing freedom of speech and political protest. Under pressure from the Allied forces, however, during World War II, Reza Shah was compelled to abdicate. Under the rule of his son, Mohammad Reza Shah Pahlavi, Iran saw greater press and political freedoms and increased economic activity. Mohammad Mosaddeq—a lawyer and political opponent of the shah who sought to curb the power of both the ulama and the monarchy—won election as prime minister in 1951, shortly after spearheading the passage of an oil nationalization act. Although the shah fled the country in 1953, a CIA-backed coup quickly toppled Mosaddeq and returned the shah to power.

The early 1960s saw an important turning point in Iran when the shah undertook an ambitious program of reform. Religious conservatives opposed such liberalizing policies, however, and feared accelerated erosion of their power. In 1963, one opponent—Ruhollah Khomeini—spoke out against these reforms, eliciting a harsh governmental response; he was arrested and later exiled. Economic and political grievances informed an opposition to the shah so broad-based that secular intellectuals opposed to the power of the clerics now imagined that, with their help, the shah could be overthrown. Newspaper remarks insulting Khomeini provided an immediate spark, and in January 1978, thousands of religious students, joined by thousands of other youths, took to the streets to protest the regime. Finally, in January 1979, the shah fled, and the following month Khomeini returned to Iran. In April, the country was declared an Islamic republic.

The establishment of the Islamic republic was followed by a chaotic period in which militias proliferated, and efforts to suppress Western influence drove much of the Western-educated elite from the country. Antiwestern sentiment culminated in the 1979 seizure of the U.S. embassy in Tehrān, an event that severely hampered U.S.-Iranian relations. For much of the 1980s, Iran was embroiled in war with Iraq, to the detriment of both countries. A cease-fire was accepted in mid-1988, shortly before Khomeini's death the following year.

With the death of Khomeini, then-president Ali Khamenei became supreme leader, and the powerful Majles speaker Ali Akbar Hashemi Rafsanjani in turn became president. Although some hoped that the pragmatic Rafsanjani might effect economic liberalization and improved relations with the West, the opposition of both Khamenei and the Majles stifled the success of his programs.

Conflict between conservative and moderate elements continued to be an important theme in Iran into the 21st century. Hope among reformers, sparked by the election of Mohammad Khatami in 1997, was tempered by Khamenei's continued opposition to his reforms. Although Khatami was reelected in 2001, confidence in his ability to cultivate change had diminished, and with the election of Mahmoud Ahmadinejad in 2005, conservative elements retook the presidency. Ahmadinejad pursued confrontational policies toward the West that impaired that relationship in later years, and, in spite of an outpouring of apparent popular opposition to Ahmadinejad, he was reelected in mid-2009.

With the unrest that accompanied the 2009 election, some observers perceived Iran at a crossroads where the balance between moderates and conservatives might be subject to revision. In a country where the populace had effected change through popular protest before, at the end of the first decade of the 21st century, many were left wondering how recent events might effect both the people of Iran and the country's broader political system.

CHAPTER 1

LAND

Iran is a mountainous, arid, ethnically diverse country of southwestern Asia. Much of Iran consists of a central desert plateau, which is ringed on all sides by lofty mountain ranges that afford access to the interior through high passes. Most of the population lives on the edges of this forbidding, waterless waste. The capital is Tehrān, a sprawling, jumbled metropolis at the southern foot of the Elburz (Alborz) Mountains.

Irån, Encyclopædia Britannica, Inc.

Iran is bounded to the north by Azerbaijan, Armenia, Turkmenistan, and the Caspian Sea, to the east by Pakistan and Afghanistan, to the south by the Persian Gulf and the Gulf of Oman, and to the west by Turkey and Iraq. Iran also controls about a dozen islands in the Persian Gulf. About one-third of its 4,770-mile (7,680-km) boundary is seacoast.

RELIEF

A series of massive, heavily eroded mountain ranges surrounds Iran's high interior basin. Most of the country is above 1,500 feet (460 metres), with one-sixth of it over 6,500 feet (1,980 metres). In sharp contrast are the coastal regions outside the mountain ring. In the north a strip 400 miles (650 km) long bordering the Caspian Sea and never more than 70 miles (115 km) wide (and frequently narrower) falls sharply from 10,000-foot (3,000-metre) summits to the marshy lake's edge, some 90 feet (30 metres) below sea level. Along the southern coast the land drops away from a 2,000-foot (600-metre) plateau, backed by a rugged escarpment three times as high, to meet the Persian Gulf and the Gulf of Oman.

The Zagros (Zāgros) Mountains stretch from the border with Armenia in the northwest to the Persian Gulf and thence eastward into the Baluchistan (Balūchestān) region. Farther to the south the range broadens into a band of parallel ridges 125 miles (200 km) wide that lies between the plains of Mesopotamia and the great central plateau of Iran. The range is drained on the west by streams that cut deep, narrow gorges and water fertile valleys. The land is extremely rugged and difficult to access, and is populated largely by pastoral nomads.

The Elburz Mountains run along the south shore of the Caspian Sea to meet the border ranges of the

Khorāsān region to the east. The tallest of the chain's many volcanic peaks, some of which are still active, is snow-clad Mount Damāvand (Demavend), which is also Iran's highest point. Many parts of Iran are isolated and poorly surveyed, and the elevation of many of its peaks are still in dispute; the height of Mount Damāvand is generally given as 18,605 feet (5,671 metres).

The Zagros Mountains rise above pasturelands, southwestern Iran. Fred J. Maroon/ Photo Researchers

Volcanic and Tectonic Activity

Mount Taftān, a massive cone reaching 13,261 feet (4,042 metres) in southeastern Iran, emits gas and mud at sporadic intervals. In the north, however, Mount Damāvand has been inactive in historical times, as have Mount Sabalān (15,787 feet [4,812 metres]) and Mount Sahand (12,172 feet [3,710 metres]) in the northwest. The volcanic belt extends some 1,200 miles (1,900 km) from the border with Azerbaijan in the northwest to Baluchistan in the southeast. In addition, in the northwestern section of the country, lava and ashes cover a 200-mile (320-km) stretch of land from Jolfā on the border with Azerbaijan eastward to the Caspian Sea. A third volcanic region, which is 250 miles (400 km) long and 40 miles (65 km) wide, runs between Lake Urmia (Orūmiyyeh) and the city of Qazvīn.

Earthquake activity is frequent and violent throughout the country. During the 20th century—when reliable records were available—there were fully a dozen earthquakes of 7.0 or higher on the Richter scale that took large numbers of lives. In 1990 as many as 50,000 people were killed by a powerful tremor in the Qazvīn-Zanjān area. In 2003 a relatively weak quake struck the ancient town of Bam in eastern Kermān province, leveling the town and destroying a historic fortress. More than 25,000 people perished.

Mount Damāvand

Mount Damāvand (also spelled Demavend, Persian: Qolleh-ye Damāvand) is an extinct volcanic peak of the Elburz Mountains, about 42 miles (68 km) northeast of Tehrān, in northern Iran. Estimates of its height vary from about 18,400 feet (5,600 metres) to more than 19,000 feet (5,800 metres), and it dominates the surrounding ranges by 3,000 to 8,000 feet (900 to 2,450 metres). Its steep, snowcapped cone is formed of lava flows and ash and is crowned by a small crater with sulfuric deposits. Below the crater are two small glaciers. There also are fumaroles (holes for escaping fumes and gases), hot springs, and mineral deposits of travertine. Mount Damāvand is mentioned in several Persian legends, one of which gives it as the resting place of Noah's ark.

Mount Damāvand, the highest peak in the Elburz Mountains, Iran. The J. Allan Cash Photolibrary

THE INTERIOR PLATEAU

The arid interior plateau, which extends into Central Asia, is cut by several smaller mountain ranges, the largest being the Kopet-Dag (Koppeh Dāgh) Range. In the flatlands lie the plateau's most remarkable features, the Kavīr and Lūt deserts, also called Kavīr-e Lūt. At the lowest elevations, series of basins in the poorly drained soil remain dry for months at a time. The evaporation of any accumulated water produces the salt wastes known as *kavīr*s. As elevation rises, surfaces of sand and gravelly soil gradually merge into fertile soil on the hillsides and mountain slopes.

DRAINAGE

The few streams emptying into the desiccated central plateau dissipate in saline marshes. The general drainage pattern is down the outward slopes of the mountains, terminating in the sea. There are three large rivers, but only one—the Kārūn—is navigable. It originates in the Zagros Mountains and flows south to the Shatt al-Arab (Arvand Rūd), which empties into the Persian Gulf. The Sefīd (Safid) River originates in the Elburz Mountains in the north and runs as a mountain stream for most of its

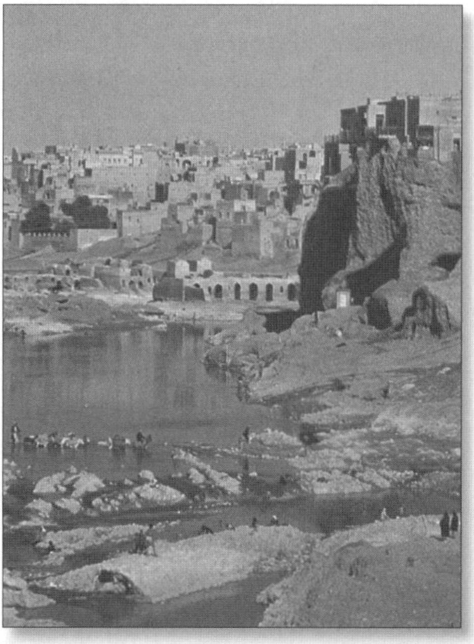

Dezfūl, on the east bank of the Dez River, Iran. Fred J. Maroon—Photo Researchers

length but flows rapidly into the Gīlān plain and then to the Caspian Sea. The Dez Dam in Dezfūl is one of the largest in the Middle East. The Sefīd River Dam, completed in the early 1960s at Manjīl, generates hydroelectric power and provides water for irrigation.

Dam on the Kārūn River, Iran. Dennis Briskin/Tom Stack & Associates

The Zāyandeh River, the lifeline of Eṣfahān province, also originates in the Zagros Mountains, flowing southeastward to Gāv Khūnī Marsh (Gāvkhāneh Lake), a swamp northwest of the city of Yazd. The completion of the Kūhrang Dam in 1971 diverted water from the upper Kārūn through a tunnel 2 miles (3 km) long into the Zāyandeh for irrigation purposes.

Other streams are seasonal and variable. Spring floods do enormous damage, while in summer many streams disappear. However, water is stored naturally underground, finding its outlet in springs and tap wells.

The largest inland body of water, Lake Urmia, in northwestern Iran, covers an area that varies from about 2,000 to 2,300 square miles (5,200 to 6,000 square km). Other lakes are principally seasonal, and all have a high salt content.

Kārūn River

The Kārūn River (Persian: Rūd-e Kārūn, known in ancient times as Ulai, or Eulaeus) is a river in southwestern Iran and a tributary of the Shatt al-Arab, which it joins at Khorramshahr. It rises in the Bakhtīārī Mountains west of Eṣfahān and follows a tortuous course trending basically southwest. The Kārūn's total length is 515 miles (829 km), though the direct distance from its source to the junction with the Shatt al-Arab is only 180 miles (290 km). Its catchment basin up to Ahvāz has an area of 22,069 square miles (57,059 square km), of which 7,000 square miles (18,130 square km) belong to its main tributary, the Dez. Most of the area is mountainous, forming part of the limestone Zagros ranges.

The river's course divides into three parts: from the sources to Gatvand, where the river emerges from the mountains; from Gatvand to Band-e Qīr, where it is joined by the Dez; and from Band-e Qīr through Ahvāz southward to the Shatt al-Arab. In its upper course the Kārūn is a powerful stream, increasing in volume as it is successively joined by its tributaries. For long stretches it flows rapidly between high precipices. At Band-e Qīr, the river, enlarged by the Dez, is navigable to its mouth except for about 2 miles (3 km) of rapids at Ahvāz. Below Ahvāz the river is sometimes too shallow for navigation, especially during the dry season. Seasonal variation in discharge rate shows the lowest water level to be in October, and the highest, as the result of combined precipitation and meltwater, in April.

Formerly the Kārūn had a lower course that was separated from and to the east of the Shatt al-Arab. In 1765, however, the river changed to its present course through the apparently artificial Ḥaffār Channel. According to the geographer al-Maqdisī, this channel was dug in 986 CE to facilitate water communication between Ahvāz and Basra. This change resulted in frontier disputes between the Ottoman Empire and Iran, disputes that were settled by the treaty of Erzurum (1847), giving Iran access to the eastern bank of the Shatt al-Arab and the right to use the waterway.

The Kārūn up to Ahvāz was opened to international navigation in 1888, and boat services were later established between Ahvāz and Band-e Qīr. Shipping on the lower course of the Kārūn has become increasingly important owing to oil drilling and refining in the vicinity. A dam and tunnel on the river were completed in 1971 to increase the water supply of Eṣfahān.

SOILS

Soil patterns in Iran vary widely. The abundant subtropical vegetation of the Caspian coastal region is supported by rich brown forest soils. Mountain soils are shallow layers over bedrock, with a high proportion of unweathered fragments. Natural erosion moves the finer-textured soils into the valleys. The alluvial deposits are mostly chalky, and many are used for pottery. The semiarid plateaus lying above 3,000 feet (900 metres) are covered by brown or chestnut-coloured soil that supports grassy vegetation. The soil is slightly alkaline and contains 3 to 4 percent organic material. The saline and alkaline soils in the arid regions are light in colour and infertile. The sand dunes are composed of loose quartz and fragments of other minerals and, except where anchored by vegetation, are in almost constant motion, driven by high winds.

CLIMATE

Iran's climate ranges from subtropical to subpolar. In winter a high-pressure belt, centred in Siberia, slashes west and south to the interior of the Iranian plateau, and low-pressure systems develop over the warm waters of the Caspian Sea, the Persian Gulf, and the Mediterranean Sea. In summer one of the world's lowest-pressure centres prevails in the south. Low-pressure systems in Pakistan generate two regular wind patterns: the *shamāl*, which blows from February to October northwesterly through the Tigris-Euphrates valley; and the "120-day" summer wind, which can reach velocities of 70 miles (110 km) per hour in the Sīstān region near Pakistan. Warm Arabian winds bring heavy moisture from the Persian Gulf.

Elevation, latitude, maritime influences, seasonal winds, and proximity to mountain ranges or deserts play a significant role in diurnal and seasonal temperature fluctuation. The average daytime summer temperature in Ābādān in Khūzestān province tops 110 °F (43 °C), and the average daytime winter high in Tabrīz in the East Āz̄arbāyjān province barely reaches freezing. Precipitation also varies widely, from less than 2 inches (50 mm) in the southeast to about 78 inches (1,980 mm) in the Caspian region. The annual average is about 16 inches (400 mm). Winter is normally the rainy season for the country; more than half of the annual precipitation occurs in that three-month period.

The northern coastal region presents a sharp contrast. The high Elburz Mountains, which seal off the narrow

Caspian plain from the rest of the country, wring moisture from the clouds, trap humidity from the air, and create a fertile semitropical region of luxuriant forests, swamps, and rice paddies. Temperatures there may soar to 100 °F (38 °C) and the humidity to nearly 100 percent, while frosts are extremely rare. Except in this region, summer is a dry season. The northern and western parts of Iran have four distinct seasons. Toward the south and east, spring and autumn become increasingly short and ultimately merge in an area of mild winters and hot summers.

PLANT AND ANIMAL LIFE

Topography, elevation, water supply, and soil determine the character of the vegetation. Approximately one-tenth of Iran is forested, most extensively in the Caspian region. In the area are found broad-leaved deciduous trees—oak, beech, linden, elm, walnut, ash, and hornbeam—and a few broad-leaved evergreens. Thorny shrubs and ferns also abound. The Zagros Mountains are covered by scrub oak forests, together with elm, maple, hackberry, walnut, pear, and pistachio trees. Willow, poplar, and plane trees grow in the ravines, as do many species of creepers. Thin stands of juniper, almond, barberry, cotoneaster, and wild fruit trees grow on the intermediate dry plateau. Thorny shrubs form the ground cover of the steppes, while species of *Artemisia* (wormwood) grow at medium elevations of the desert plains and the rolling country. Acacia, dwarf palm, *kunar* trees (of the genus *Ziziphus*), and scattered shrubs are found below 3,000 feet (900 metres). Desert sand dunes, which hold water, support thickets of brush. Forests follow the courses of surface or subterranean waters. Oases support vines and tamarisk, poplar, date palm, myrtle, oleander, acacia, willow, elm, plum, and mulberry trees. In swamp areas reeds and grass provide good pasture.

Date Palm

The date palm (*Phoenix dactylifera*) is a tree of the palm family (Arecaceae, or Palmae), found in the Canary Islands, northern Africa, the Middle East, Pakistan, India, and the U.S. state of California. The date palm grows about 75 feet (23 metres) tall. Its stem, strongly marked with the pruned stubs of old leaf bases, terminates in a crown of graceful, shining, pinnate leaves about 16 feet (5 metres) long. Floral spikes branch from the axils of leaves that emerged the previous year.

Male and female flowers are borne on separate plants. Under cultivation the female flowers are artificially pollinated. The date is a one-seeded fruit, or berry, usually oblong but varying much in shape, size, colour, quality, and consistency of flesh, according to the conditions of culture. More than 1,000 dates may appear on a single bunch weighing 8 kg (18 pounds) or more. The dried fruit is more than 50 percent sugar by weight and contains about 2 percent each of protein, fat, and mineral matter.

Ripening dates, fruit of the date palm (Phoenix dactylifera). Grant Heilman Photography

The date palm has been cultivated and prized from remotest antiquity; its fruit has been the staple food and chief source of wealth in the irrigable deserts of North Africa and the Middle East. Spanish missionaries carried the tree to the New World in the 18th and early 19th centuries.

All parts of the date palm yield products of economic value. Its trunk furnishes timber; the midribs of the leaves supply material for crates and furniture; the leaflets, for basketry; the leaf bases, for fuel; the fruit stalks, for rope and fuel; the fibre, for cordage and packing material; and the seeds are sometimes ground and used as stock feed. Syrup, alcohol, vinegar, and a strong liquor are derived from the fruit. The sap is also used as a beverage, either fresh or fermented, but because the method of extraction seriously injures the palm, only those trees that produce little fruit are used for sap. When a palm is cut down, the tender terminal bud is eaten as a salad.

Saudi Arabia, Egypt, Iran, and Iraq are the leading date-producing and exporting countries, although fruit from Algeria and Tunisia also is well known in Europe. California is the major American producer.

Wildlife includes leopards, bears, hyenas, wild boars, ibex, gazelles, and mouflons, which live in the wooded mountains. Jackals and rabbits are common in the country's interior. Wild asses live in the *kavīr*s. Cheetahs and pheasants are found in the Caspian region, and partridges live in most parts of the country. Aquatic birds such as seagulls, ducks, and geese live on the shores of the Caspian Sea and the Persian Gulf, while buzzards nest in the desert. Deer, hedgehogs, foxes, and more than 20 species of rodents live in semidesert, high-elevation regions. Palm squirrels, Asiatic black bears, and tigers are found in Baluchistan. Tigers also once inhabited the forests of the Caspian region but are now assumed to be extinct.

Studies made in Khūzestān province and the Baluchistan region and along the slopes of the Elburz and Zagros mountains have revealed the presence of a remarkably wide variety of amphibians and reptiles. Examples are toads, frogs, tortoises, lizards, salamanders, boas, racers, rat snakes (*Ptyas*), cat snakes (*Tarbophis fallax*), and vipers.

Some 200 varieties of fish live in the Persian Gulf, as do shrimps, lobsters, and turtles. Sturgeon, the most important commercial fish, is one of 30 species found in the Caspian Sea. It constitutes a major source of export income for the government, in the production of caviar. Mountain trout abound in small streams at high elevations and in rivers that are not seasonal.

The government has established wildlife sanctuaries such as the Bakhtegān Wildlife Refuge, Tūrān Protected Area, and Golestān National Park. The hunting of swans, pheasants, deer, tigers, and a number of other animals and birds is prohibited.

CHAPTER 2

People

Iran is a culturally diverse society, and interethnic relations are generally amicable. The predominant ethnic and cultural group in the country consists of native speakers of Persian. But the people who are generally known as Persians are of mixed ancestry, and the country has important Turkic and Arab elements in addition to the Kurds, Baloch, Bakhtyārī, Lurs, and other smaller minorities (Armenians, Assyrians, Jews, Brahuis, and others).

ETHNIC GROUPS

The Persians, Kurds, and speakers of other Indo-European languages in Iran are descendants of the Aryan tribes that began migrating from Central Asia into what is now Iran in the 2nd millennium BCE. Those of Turkic ancestry are the descendants of tribes that appeared in the region—also from Central Asia—beginning in the 11th century CE, and the Arab minority settled predominantly in the country's southwest (in Khūzestān, a region also known as Arabistan) following the Islamic conquests of the 7th century. Like the Persians, many of Iran's smaller ethnic groups chart their arrival into the region to ancient times.

The Kurds have been both urban and rural (with a significant portion of the latter at times nomadic), and they are concentrated in the western mountains of Iran. This group, which constitutes only a small proportion of Iran's population, has resisted the Iranian government's efforts, both before and after the revolution of 1979, to assimilate them into the mainstream of national life and, along with their fellow Kurds in adjacent regions of Iraq and Turkey, has sought either regional autonomy or the outright establishment of an independent Kurdish state in the region.

Also inhabiting the western mountains are seminomadic Lurs, thought to be the descendants of the aboriginal inhabitants of the country. Closely related are the Bakhtyārī tribes, who live in the Zagros Mountains west of Eṣfahān. The Baloch are a smaller minority who inhabit Iranian Baluchistan, which borders on Pakistan.

Cloth being woven by Qashqā'ī women in the area of Shīrāz, Iran. © R. & S. Michaud/Woodfin Camp & Associates

The largest Turkic group is the Azerbaijanians, a farming and herding people who inhabit two border provinces in the northwestern corner of Iran. Two other Turkic ethnic groups are the Qashqā'ī, in the Shīrāz area to the north of the Persian Gulf, and the Turkmen, of Khorāsān in the northeast.

The Armenians, with a different ethnic heritage, are concentrated in Tehrān, Eṣfahān, and the Azerbaijan region and are engaged primarily in commercial pursuits. A few isolated groups speaking Dravidian dialects are found in the Sīstān region to the southeast.

Semites—Jews, Assyrians, and Arabs—constitute only a small percentage of the population. The Jews trace their heritage in Iran to the Babylonian Exile of the 6th century BCE and, like the Armenians, have retained their ethnic, linguistic, and religious identity. Both groups traditionally have clustered in the largest cities. The Assyrians are concentrated in the northwest, and the Arabs live in Khūzestān as well as in the Persian Gulf islands.

LANGUAGES

Although Persian (Farsi) is the predominant and official language of Iran, a number of languages and dialects from three language families—Indo-European, Altaic, and Afro-Asiatic—are spoken.

Roughly three-fourths of Iranians speak one of the Indo-European languages. Slightly more than half the population speak a dialect of Persian, an Iranian language of the Indo-Iranian group. Literary Persian, the language's more refined variant, is understood to some degree by most Iranians. Persian is also the predominant language of literature, journalism, and the sciences. Less than one-tenth of the population speaks Kurdish. The Lurs and Bakhtyārī both speak Lurī, a language distinct from, but closely related to, Persian. Armenian, a single language of the Indo-European family, is spoken only by the Armenian minority.

The Altaic family is represented overwhelmingly by the Turkic languages, which are spoken by roughly one-fourth of the population; most speak Azerbaijanian, a language similar to modern Turkish. The Turkmen language, another Turkic language, is spoken in Iran by only a small number of Turkmen.

Of the Semitic languages—from the Afro-Asiatic family—Arabic is the most widely spoken, but only a small percentage of the population speaks it as a native tongue. The main importance of the Arabic language in Iran is historical and religious. Following the Islamic conquest of Persia, Arabic virtually subsumed Persian as a literary tongue. Since that time Persian has adopted a large number of Arabic words—perhaps one-third or more of its lexicon—and borrowed grammatical constructions from Classical and, in some instances, colloquial Arabic. Under the monarchy, efforts were made to purge Arabic elements from the Persian language, but these met with little success and ceased outright following the revolution. Since that time, the study of Classical Arabic, the language of the Qur'ān, has been emphasized in schools, and Arabic remains the predominant language of learned religious discourse.

Before 1979, English and French, and to a lesser degree German and Russian, were widely used by the educated class. European languages are used less commonly but are still taught at schools and universities.

Persian Language

Persian, also called Farsi, is a member of the Iranian branch of the Indo-Iranian language family and is the official language of Iran. It is most closely related to Middle and Old Persian, former languages of the region of Fārs ("Persia") in southwestern Iran. Modern Persian is thus called Farsi by native speakers. Written in Arabic script, modern Persian also has many Arabic loanwords and an extensive literature.

Old Persian, spoken until approximately the 3rd century BCE, is attested by numerous inscriptions written in cuneiform, most notable of which is the great monument of Darius I at Bīsitūn, Iran. The inscriptions at Bīsitūn were generally trilingual—in Old Persian, Elamite, and Akkadian.

Middle Persian, spoken from the 3rd century BCE to the 9th century CE, is represented by numerous epigraphic texts of Sāsānian kings, written in Aramaic script; there is also a varied literature in Middle Persian embracing both the Zoroastrian and the Manichaean religious traditions. Pahlavi was the name of the official Middle Persian language of the Sāsānian empire.

Modern Persian grammar is in many ways much simpler than its ancestral forms, having lost most of the inflectional systems of the older varieties of Persian. Other than markers to indicate that nouns and pronouns are direct objects, Modern Persian has no system of case inflections. Possession is shown by addition of a special suffix (called the *ezāfeh*) to the possessed noun. Verbs retain a set of personal endings related to those of other Indo-European languages, but a series of prefixes and infixes (word elements inserted within a word), as well as auxiliary verbs, are used instead of a single complex inflectional system in order to mark tense, mood, voice, and the negative.

RELIGION

The vast majority of Iranians are Muslims of the Ithnā ʿAsharī, or Twelver, Shīʿite branch, which is the official state religion. The Kurds and Turkmen are predominantly Sunni Muslims, but Iran's Arabs are both Sunni and Shīʿite. Small communities of Christians, Jews, and Zoroastrians are also found throughout the country.

Shīʿism

The two cornerstones of Iranian Shīʿism are the promise of the return of the divinely inspired 12th imam—Muḥammad al-Mahdī al-Ḥujjah, whom Shīʿites believe to be the mahdi—and the veneration of his martyred forebears. The absence of the imam contributed indirectly to the development in modern Iran of a strong Shīʿite clergy whose penchant for status, particularly in the 20th century, led to a proliferation of titles and honorifics unique in the Islamic world. The Shīʿite clergy have been the predominant political and social force in Iran since the Islamic revolution.

Mahdi

In Islamic eschatology the mahdi (Arabic: "divinely guided one") is a messianic deliverer who will fill the Earth with justice and equity, restore true religion, and usher in a short golden age lasting seven, eight, or nine years before the end of the world. The Qur'ān (Islamic sacred scriptures) does not mention him, and almost no reliable hadith (saying attributed to the Prophet Muhammad) concerning the mahdi can be adduced. Many Sunnī theologians accordingly question mahdist beliefs, but such beliefs form a necessary part of Shīʿite doctrine.

The doctrine of the mahdi seems to have gained currency during the confusion and insecurity of the religious and political upheavals of early Islam (7th and 8th centuries). In 686 al-Mukhtār ibn Abū ʿUbayd at-Thaqafī, leader of a revolt of non-Arab Muslims in Iraq, seems to have first used the doctrine by maintaining his allegiance to a son of ʿAlī (Muhammad's son-in-law and fourth caliph), Muḥammad ibn al-Ḥanafiyyah, even after al-Ḥanafiyyah's death. Abū ʿUbayd taught that, as mahdi, al-Ḥanafiyyah remained alive in his tomb in a state of occultation (*ghaybah*) and would reappear to vanquish his enemies. In 750 the ʿAbbāsid revolution made use of eschatological prophecies current at the time that the mahdi would rise in Khorāsān in the east, carrying a black banner.

Belief in the mahdi has tended to receive new emphasis in every time of crisis. Thus, after the battle of Las Navas de Tolosa (1212), when most of Spain was lost for Islam, Spanish Muslims circulated traditions ascribed to the Prophet foretelling a reconquest of Spain by the mahdi. During the Napoleonic invasion of Egypt, a person claiming to be the mahdi appeared briefly in Lower Egypt.

Because the mahdi is seen as a restorer of the political power and religious purity of Islam, the title has tended to be claimed by social revolutionaries in Islamic society. North Africa in particular has seen a number of self-styled mahdis, most important of these being ʿUbayd Allāh, founder of the Fāṭimid dynasty (909); Muḥammad ibn Tūmart, founder of the Almohad movement in Morocco in the 12th century; and Muḥammad Aḥmad, the mahdi of the Sudan who, in 1881, revolted against the Egyptian administration.

Clergy

There is no concept of ordination in Islam. Hence, the role of clergy is played not by a priesthood but by a community of scholars called the ulama (Arabic: *'ulamā'*). To become a member of the Shīʿite ulama, a male Muslim need only attend a traditional Islamic college, or madrasah. The main course of study in such an institution is Islamic jurisprudence (Arabic: *fiqh*), but a student need not complete his madrasah studies to become a *faqīh*, or jurist. In Iran such a low-level clergyman is generally referred to by the generic term *mullah* (Arabic: *al-mawlā*, "lord"; Persian: *mullā*) or *ākhūnd* or, more recently, *rūḥānī* (Persian: "spiritual"). To become a mullah, one need merely advance to a level of scholarly competence recognized by other members of the clergy. Mullahs staff the vast majority of local religious posts in Iran.

The Arabesque dome of the Māder-e Shah madrasah, Esfahān, Iran. Ray Manley/Shostal Associates

An aspirant gains the higher status of *mujtahid*—a scholar competent to practice independent reasoning in legal judgement (Arabic: *ijtihād*)—by first graduating from a recognized madrasah and obtaining the general recognition of his peers and then, most important, by gaining a substantial following among the Shīʿite community. A contender for this status is ordinarily referred to by the honorific *hojatoleslām* (Arabic: *ḥujjat al-Islām*, "proof of Islam"). Few clergymen are eventually recognized as *mujtahid*s, and some are honoured by the term *ayatollah* (Arabic: *āyat Allāh*, "sign of God"). The honorific of grand ayatollah (*āyat Allāh al-ʿuẓmā*) is conferred only upon those Shīʿite *mujtahid*s whose level of insight and expertise in Islamic canon law has risen to the level of one who is worthy of being a *marjaʿ-e taqlīd* (Arabic: *marjaʿ al-taqlīd*, "model of emulation"), the highest level of excellence in Iranian Shīʿism.

There is no real religious hierarchy or infrastructure within Shīʿism, and scholars often hold independent and varied views on political, social, and religious issues. Hence, these honorifics are not awarded but attained by scholars through general consensus and popular appeal. Shīʿites of every level defer to clergymen on the basis of their reputation for learning and judicial acumen, and the trend has become strong in modern Shīʿism for every believer, in order to avoid sin, to follow the teachings of his or her chosen *marjaʿ-e taqlīd*. This has increased the power of the ulama in Iran, and it has also enhanced their role as mediators to the divine in a way not seen in Sunni Islam or in earlier Shīʿism.

Sayyids

Those of the family of Muhammad who are not his direct descendents through the line of the 12th imam are referred to as sayyids. These individuals have traditionally been viewed with a high degree of reverence by believing Iranians and continue to have strong influence in contemporary Iranian culture. Many sayyids are found among the clergy, although in modern Iran they may practice virtually any occupation.

Religious Minorities

Christians, Jews, and Zoroastrians are the most significant religious minorities in Iran. Christians are the most numerous group of these, Orthodox Armenians constituting the bulk. The Assyrians are Nestorian, Protestant, and Roman Catholic, as are a few converts from other ethnic groups. The Zoroastrians are largely concentrated in Yazd in central Iran, Kermān in the southeast, and Tehrān.

Religious toleration, one of the characteristics of Iran during the Pahlavi monarchy, came to an end with the Islamic revolution in 1978–79. While Christians, Jews, and Zoroastrians are recognized in the constitution of 1979 as official minorities, the revolutionary atmosphere in Iran was not conducive to equal treatment of non-Muslims. Among these, members of the Bahā'ī faith—a religion founded in Iran—were the victims of the greatest persecution. The Jewish population, which had been significant before 1979, emigrated in great numbers after the revolution.

Bahā'ī Faith

The Bahā'ī faith is a religion founded in Iran in the mid-19th century by Mīrzā Ḥoseyn 'Alī Nūrī, who is known as Bahā' Ullāh (Arabic: "Glory of God"). The cornerstone of Bahā'ī belief is the conviction that Bahā' Ullāh and his forerunner, who was known as the Bāb, were manifestations of God, who in his essence is unknowable. The principal Bahā'ī tenets are the essential unity of all religions and the unity of humanity. Bahā'īs believe that all the founders of the world's great religions have been manifestations of God and agents of a progressive divine plan for the education of the human race. In spite of their apparent differences, the world's great religions, according to the Bahā'īs, teach an identical truth. Bahā' Ullāh's

Bahā'ī House of Worship, Wilmette, Ill. Francisco Gonzalez/© Baha'i International Community

peculiar function was to overcome the disunity of religions and establish a universal faith.

Bahā'īs believe in the oneness of humanity and devote themselves to the abolition of racial, class, and religious prejudices. The great bulk of Bahā'ī teachings is concerned with social ethics. The faith has no priesthood and does not observe ritual forms in its worship.

The Bahā'ī faith underwent a rapid expansion beginning in the 1960s, and by the late 20th century it had more than 150 national spiritual assemblies (national governing bodies) and about 20,000 local spiritual assemblies. After Islamic fundamentalists came to power in Iran in 1979, the 300,000 Bahā'īs there were persecuted by the government.

SETTLEMENT PATTERNS

Topography and water supply determine the regions fit for human habitation, the lifestyles of the people, and the types of dwellings. The deep gorges and defiles, unnavigable rivers, empty deserts, and impenetrable *kavīrs* have all contributed to insularity and tribalism among the Iranian peoples, and the population has become concentrated around the periphery of the interior plateau and in the oases. The felt yurts of the Turkmen, the black tents of the Bakhtyārī, and the osier huts of the Baloch are typical, as the tribespeople roam from summer to winter pastures. The vast central and southern plains are dotted with numerous oasis settlements with scattered rudimentary hemispherical or conical huts. Since the mid-20th century the migrations have shortened, and the nomads have settled in more permanent villages.

Mosque with cupola in the bazaar, Tehrān, Iran. Margot Wolf—SCALA/Art Resource, New York

The villages on the plains follow an ancient rectangular pattern. High mud walls with corner towers form the outer face of the houses, which have flat roofs of mud and straw supported by wooden rafters. A mosque is situated in the open centre of the village and serves also as a school.

Mountain villages are situated on the rocky slopes above the valley floor, surrounded by terraced fields (usually irrigated) in which grain and alfalfa (lucerne) are raised. The houses are square, mud-brick, windowless buildings with flat or domed roofs; a roof hole provides ventilation and light. Houses are usually two stories high, with a stable occupying the ground floor.

Caspian villages are different from those of both the plains and the mountains. The scattered hamlets typically consist of two-storied wooden houses. Separate outbuildings (barns, henhouses, silkworm houses) surround an open courtyard.

The majority of the urban population is concentrated on Tehrān, the capital of Iran and its largest city, which is separated from the Caspian Sea by the Elburz Mountains. Eṣfahān, about 250 miles (400 km) south of Tehrān, is the

The Niāvarān Palace, Tehrān, Iran. Robert Harding Picture Library

second most important city and is famed for its architecture. There are few cities in central and eastern Iran, where water is scarce, although lines of oases penetrate the desert. Most towns are supplied with water by *qanāt*, an irrigation system by which an underground mountain water source is tapped and the water channeled down through a series of tunnels, sometimes 50 miles (80 km) in length, to the town level. Towns are, therefore, often located a short distance from the foot of a mountain. The essential feature of a traditional Iranian street is a small canal.

City layout is typical of Islamic communities. The various sectors of society—governmental, residential, and business—are often divided into separate quarters. The business quarter, or bazaar, fronting on a central square, is a maze of narrow arcades lined with small individual shops grouped according to the type of product sold. Modern business centres, however, have grown up outside the bazaars. Dwellings in the traditional style—consisting of domed-roof structures constructed of mud-brick or stone—are built around closed courtyards, with a garden and a pool. Public baths are found in all sections of the cities.

Construction of broad avenues and ring roads to accommodate modern traffic has changed the appearance of the large cities. Their basic plan, however, is still that of a labyrinth of narrow, crooked streets and culs-de-sac.

DEMOGRAPHIC TRENDS

Iran is a young country. One-fourth of its people are 15 years of age or younger, and well over half are under age 30. However, the country's postrevolutionary boom in births has slowed substantially, and—with a birth below the world average and a low death rate—Iran's natural rate of increase is now only marginally higher than the world average. Life expectancy in Iran is some 68 years for men and 71 years for women.

Internal migration from rural areas to cities was a major trend beginning in the 1960s (nearly three-fourths of Iranians are defined as urban), but the most significant demographic phenomenon following the revolution in 1979 was the out-migration of a large portion of the educated, secularized population to Western countries, particularly to the United States. (Several hundred thousand Iranians had settled in southern California alone by the end of the 20th century.) Likewise, a considerable number of religious minorities, mostly Jews and Bahāʾīs, have left the country—either as emigrants or asylum seekers—because of unfavourable political conditions. Internally, migration to the cities has continued, and Iran has absorbed large numbers of refugees from neighbouring Afghanistan (mostly Persian [Dari]-speaking Afghans) and Iraq (both Arabs and Kurds).

CHAPTER 3

Economy

The most formidable hurdle facing Iran's economy remains its continuing isolation from the international community, which has hampered the short- and long-term growth of its markets, restricted the country's access to high technology, and impeded foreign investment. Iran's isolation is a product both of the xenophobia of its more conservative politicians—who fear postimperial entanglements—and sanctions imposed by the international community, particularly the United States, which has accused Iran of supporting international terrorism and developing an illicit nuclear program. The Iran and Libya Sanctions Act of 1996 expanded an existing U.S. embargo on the import of Iranian petroleum products to encompass extensive bans on investment both by U.S. and non-U.S. companies in Iran. These prohibitions included bans on foreign speculation in Iranian petroleum development, the export of high technology to Iran, and the import of a wide variety of Iranian products into the United States. Overtures by reform-minded Iranian politicians to open their country to foreign investment have met with limited success, but in the early 21st century U.S. sanctions remained in place.

Iran's long-term objectives since the Islamic revolution have been economic independence, full employment, and a comfortable standard of living for its citizens, but at the end of the 20th century the country's economic future was lined with obstacles. Iran's population more than doubled in that period, and its population grew increasingly young. In a country that has traditionally been both rural and agrarian, agricultural production has fallen consistently since the 1960s (by the late 1990s Iran was a major food importer), and economic hardship in the countryside has driven vast numbers of people to migrate to the largest cities. The rates of both literacy and life expectancy in Iran are high for the region, but so, too, is the unemployment rate, and inflation is regularly in the range of 20 percent annually.

Iran remains highly dependent on its one major industry, the extraction of petroleum and natural gas for export, and the government faces increasing difficulty in providing opportunities for a younger, better-educated workforce, which has led to a growing sense of frustration among lower- and middle-class Iranians. Still, the government has tried to develop the country's communication, transportation, manufacturing, and energy infrastructures (including its prospective nuclear power facilities) and has begun the process of integrating its communication and transportation systems with those of neighbouring states.

STATE PLANNING

The national constitution divides the economy into three sectors: public, which includes major industries, banks, insurance companies, utilities, communications, foreign trade, and mass transportation; cooperative, which includes production and distribution of goods and services; and private, which consists of all activities that supplement the first two sectors. The constitution also establishes specific guidelines for the administration of the nation's economic and financial resources, and after the revolution the government declared null and void any law, or section of a law, that violated Islamic principles. This prohibition restricts individuals or institutions from charging interest on loans, an action considered illegal under Islamic law, and also places limits on certain types of financial speculation. These restrictions have heretofore made Iran's participation in the international economic community problematic, which has led to harsh financial conditions and a strong reliance on local markets.

From the first years of the revolution, two different factions have sought to impose their own interpretation of Islamic economics on the government. Islamic leftists have called for extensive nationalization and expansion of a welfare state. Conservatives within the religious establishment, who have maintained strong ties to the merchant community, have defended the rights of property owners and insisted on maintaining privatization. Both factions, however, have generally supported the government's restriction on Western banking practices. Although Iran's first postrevolutionary leader, Ayatollah Ruhollah Khomeini, refused to takes sides in the leftist-conservative debate, the effects of the Iran-Iraq War (1980–88) prompted increased state intervention in the economy. The government gained a virtual monopoly over income-producing activities by nationalizing private banks and insurance companies and increasing state control of foreign trade.

REFORM

The economy continued to lag in spite of Iran's move away from public control of the financial system after the end of the war in 1990. The election of Mohammad Khatami as president in 1997 promised social and economic reform, and a number of key government positions were filled by reformist clergy and technocrats. Nonetheless, no steps have been taken on numerous proposed plans to reduce state control of the economy and encourage privatization, and the government's economic policies have remained unclear.

U.S. sanctions have also continued to hamstring Iran's economy by restricting access to Western technology, in

Iranian Pres. Mohammad Khatami addressing the crowd at a rally. Khatami's election in 1997 sparked hope among reformers, but many were disappointed when conservative opposition made it difficult for him to enact planned reforms. Atta Kenare/AFP/Getty Images

spite of the willingness of some European and East Asian companies to ignore these measures. Conservatives within Iran's government have been willing, in limited instances, to ease the restriction on interest-bearing transactions but have continued to block reformists' plans to introduce large amounts of foreign capital into the country, particularly investments from the United States. Foreign investment has remained a contentious issue because of the adverse social and political effects of foreign economic entanglements during Iran's colonial past.

AGRICULTURE, FORESTRY, AND FISHING

Roughly one-third of Iran's total surface area is arable farmland, of which less than one-fourth—or one-tenth of the total land area—is under cultivation, because of poor soil and lack of adequate water distribution in many areas. Less than one-third of the cultivated area is irrigated; the rest is devoted to dry farming. The western and northwestern portions of the country have the most fertile soils.

At the end of the 20th century, agricultural activities accounted for about one-fifth of Iran's gross domestic product (GDP) and employed a comparable proportion of the workforce. Most farms are small, less than 25 acres (10 hectares), and thus are not economically viable, which has contributed to the wide-scale migration to cities. In addition to water scarcity and areas of poor soil, seed is of low quality and farming techniques are antiquated.

All these factors have contributed to low crop yields and poverty in rural areas. Further, after the Islamic revolution many agricultural workers claimed ownership

Citrus orchards outside Kāzerūn, Iran. J.P. Vuillomenet—Rapho/Photo Researchers

rights and forcibly occupied large, privately owned farms where they had been employed. The legal disputes that arose from this situation remained unresolved through the 1980s, and many owners put off making large capital investments that would have improved farm productivity, further deteriorating production. Progressive government efforts and incentives during the 1990s, however, improved agricultural productivity marginally, helping Iran toward its goal of reestablishing national self-sufficiency in food production. The wide range of temperature fluctuation in different parts of the country and the multiplicity of climatic zones make it possible to cultivate a diverse variety of crops, including cereals (wheat, barley, rice, and corn [maize]), fruits (dates, figs, pomegranates, melons, and grapes), vegetables, cotton, sugar beets and sugarcane, nuts, olives, spices, tea, tobacco, and medicinal herbs.

Iran's forests cover approximately the same amount of land as its agricultural crops—about one-tenth of its total

Wharf at the Caspian port of Bandar-e Anzalī, Iran. Fred J. Maroon/Photo Researchers

surface area. The largest and most valuable woodland areas are in the Caspian region, where many of the forests are commercially exploitable and include both hardwoods and softwoods. Forest products include plywood, fibreboard, and lumber for the construction and furniture industries.

Fishing is also important, and Iran harvests fish both for domestic consumption and for export, marketing their products fresh, salted, smoked, or canned. Sturgeon (yielding its roe for caviar), bream, whitefish, salmon, mullet, carp, catfish, perch, and roach are caught in the Caspian Sea, Iran's most important fishery. More than 200 species of fish are found in the Persian Gulf, 150 of which are edible, including shrimps and prawns.

Dry Farming

Dry farming is the cultivation of crops without irrigation in regions of limited moisture, typically less than 20 inches (50 cm) of precipitation annually. Dry farming depends upon efficient storage of the limited moisture in the soil and the selection of crops and growing methods that make the best use of this moisture. Tilling the land shortly after harvest and keeping it free from weeds are typical methods, but in certain latitudes stubble is left in the fields after harvest to trap snow. Moisture control during crop growing consists largely of destruction of weeds and prevention of runoff. The ideal soil surface is free of weeds but has enough clods or dead vegetable matter to hinder runoff and prevent erosion.

Crops adapted to dry farming may be either drought resistant or drought evasive. Drought-resistant crops, such as sorghum, are able to reduce transpiration (emission of moisture) and may nearly cease growing during periods of moisture shortage, resuming growth when conditions again become favourable. Drought-evasive crops achieve their main growth during times of year when heat and drought conditions are not severe. Crops adapted to dry farming are usually smaller and quicker to mature than those grown under more humid conditions and are usually allotted more space.

Of the country's livestock, sheep are by far the most numerous, followed by goats, cattle, asses, horses, water buffalo, and mules. The raising of poultry for eggs and meat is prevalent, and camels are still raised and bred for use in transport.

RESOURCES AND POWER

Miners worked primarily by hand until the early 1960s, and mine owners moved the ore to refining centres by truck, rail, donkey, or camel. As public and private concerns opened new mines and quarries, they introduced mechanized methods of production. The mineral industries encompass both refining and manufacturing.

The extraction and processing of petroleum is unquestionably Iran's single most important economic activity and the most valuable in terms of revenue, although natural gas production is increasingly important. The government-operated National Iranian Oil Company (NIOC) produces petroleum for export and domestic consumption. Petroleum is moved by pipeline to the terminal of Khārk Island in the Persian Gulf and from there is shipped by tanker throughout the world. Iran's main refining facility at Ābādān was destroyed during the war with Iraq, but the government has since rebuilt the facility, and production has returned to near prewar levels. The NIOC also operates refineries at Eṣfahān, Shīrāz, Lāvān Island, Tehrān, and Tabrīz; several were damaged by Iraqi forces but have since returned to production. These sites produce a variety of refined products, including aircraft fuel at the Ābādān facility and fuels for domestic heating and the transportation industry.

Iran's vast natural gas reserves constitute more than one-tenth of the world's total. In addition to the country's working gas fields in the Elburz Mountains and in Khorāsān, fields have been discovered and exploitation begun in the Persian Gulf near 'Asalūyeh, offshore in the Caspian region, and, most notably, offshore and onshore in areas of southern Iran—the South Pars field in the latter region is one of the richest in the world. The country's gathering and distribution spur lines run to Tehrān, Kāshān, Eṣfahān, Shīrāz, Mashhad, Ahvāz, and the industrial city of Alborz, near Qazvīn. The two state-owned Iranian Gas Trunklines are the largest gas pipelines in the Middle East, and Iran is under contract to supply natural gas to Russia, eastern Europe, Pakistan, Turkey, and India through pipelines, under construction in neighbouring countries, that are intended to connect Iran's trunk lines with those of its customers.

The petrochemical industry, concentrated in the south of the country, expanded rapidly before the Islamic revolution. It, too, was largely destroyed during the Iran-Iraq War but has mostly been restored to its prewar condition. The Rāzī (formerly Shāhpūr) Petrochemical Company at Bandar-e Khomeynī (formerly Bandar-e Shāhpūr) is a subsidiary of the National Petrochemical Company of Iran and produces ammonia, phosphates, sulfur, liquid gas, and light oil.

In addition to the major coal mines found in Khorāsān, Kermān, Semnān, Māzandarān, and Gīlān, a number of smaller mines are located north of Tehrān and in Āzārbāyjān and Eṣfahān provinces. Deposits of lead, zinc, and other minerals are widely scattered throughout the country. Kermān is the centre for Iran's copper industry; deposits of copper are mined nationwide. Only since the 1990s has Iran begun to exploit such valuable minerals as uranium and gold, which it now mines and refines in commercially profitable amounts. Iran also extracts fireclay, chalk, lime, gypsum, ochre, and kaolin (china clay).

Until the 20th century, Iran's sources of energy were limited almost entirely to wood and charcoal. Petroleum, natural gas, and coal are now used to supply heat and produce the bulk of the country's electricity. A system of dams generates hydroelectric power (and also supplies water for cropland irrigation).

The Atomic Energy Organization (AEO) of Iran was established in 1973 to construct a network of more than 20 nuclear power plants. By 1978 two 1,200-megawatt reactors near Būshehr on the Persian Gulf were near completion and were scheduled to begin operation early in 1980, but the revolutionary government canceled the program in 1979. The AEO is now engaged in nuclear research and, with Russian and Chinese aid, is constructing several medium-size nuclear power reactors as well as support facilities for producing and refining uranium into fissile material.

MANUFACTURING

Tehrān is the largest market for domestic agricultural and manufactured products, which are shipped to the nearest town and thence to Tehrān and the provincial capitals by air, truck, rail, camel, mule, and donkey. Since craft production is localized, each city has created a market for its products in the capital and other major cities. Major manufacturing industries, which have transformed large parts of Iran since 1954, are scattered throughout the country, and their products are distributed nationwide.

Industrial development, which began in earnest in the mid-1950s, has transformed parts of the country. Iran now

A traditional Persian rug takes shape on a sizable loom. Carpets have been an Iranian export mainstay for centuries. Shutterstock.com

produces a wide range of manufactured commodities, such as automobiles, electric appliances, telecommunications equipment, industrial machinery, paper, rubber products, steel, food products, wood and leather products, textiles, and pharmaceuticals. Textile mills are centred in Eşfahān and along the Caspian coast. Iran is known throughout the world for its handwoven carpets. The traditional craft of making these Persian rugs contributes substantially to rural incomes and is one of Iran's most important export industries.

Until the early 1950s the construction industry was limited largely to small domestic companies. Increased income from oil and gas and the availability of easy credit, however, triggered a subsequent building boom that attracted major international construction firms to Iran. This growth continued until the mid-1970s, when, because of a sharp rise in inflation, credit was tightened and the boom collapsed. The construction industry had revived somewhat by the mid-1980s, but housing shortages have remained a serious problem, especially in the large urban centres.

FINANCE

The government makes loans and credits available to industrial and agricultural projects, primarily through banks. All private banks and insurance companies were nationalized in 1979, and the Islamic Bank of Iran (later reorganized as the Islamic Economy Organization and exempt from nationalization) was established in Tehrān, with branches throughout the country. Iran's 10 banks are divided into three categories—commercial, industrial, and agricultural—but all are subject to the same regulations. In lieu of interest on loans, considered to be usury and forbidden under Islamic law, banks impose a service charge, a commission, or both. The Central Bank of the Islamic Republic of Iran in Tehrān issues the rial, the national currency.

Islamic Banking

One of the oldest forms of bank regulation consists of laws restricting the rates of interest bankers are allowed to charge on loans or to pay on deposits. Ancient and medieval Christians held it to be immoral for a lender to earn interest from a venture that did not involve substantial risk of loss, and today Islamic law also prohibits the collection of interest. Consequently, in most Muslim countries financial intermediation is based not on debt contracts involving explicit interest payments but on profit-and-loss-sharing arrangements, in which banks and their depositors assume a share of ownership of their creditors' enterprises. (This was the case in some medieval Christian arrangements as well.) In spite of the complexity of the Islamic approach, especially with regard to contracts, effective banking systems developed as alternatives to their Western counterparts. Yet during the 1960s and early '70s, when nominal market rates of interest exceeded 20 percent in much of the world, Islamic-style banks risked being eclipsed by Western-style banks that could more readily adjust their lending terms to reflect changing market conditions. Oil revenues eventually improved the demand for Islamic banking, and by the early 21st century hundreds of Islamic-style financial institutions existed around the world, handling hundreds of billions of dollars in annual transactions. Consequently, some larger multinational banks in the West began to offer banking services consistent with Islamic law.

The strict regulation of lending rates—that is, the setting of maximum rates, or the outright prohibition of interest-taking—has been less common outside Muslim countries. Markets are far more effective than regulations at influencing interest rates, and the wide variety of loans, all of which involve differing degrees of risk, make the design and enforcement of such regulations difficult. By the 21st century most countries had stopped regulating the rate of interest paid on deposits.

TRADE

In spite of the government's attempts to make Iran economically self-sufficient, the value of the country's imports continues to be high. Foodstuffs account for a considerable proportion of total import value, followed by basic manufactures and machinery and transport equipment. The huge income derived from the export of petroleum products has generally created a favourable annual balance of trade. Other exports include carpets, fruits and nuts, chemicals, and metals. Iran's leading trading partners are Germany, Japan, and the United Kingdom.

SERVICES

In spite of efforts in the 1990s toward economic liberalization, government spending—including expenditures by quasi-governmental foundations that dominate the economy—has been high. Estimates of service sector spending in Iran are regularly more than two-fifths of the GDP, and much of that is government-related spending, including military expenditures, government salaries, and social service disbursements.

Until the early 1960s, little attention was paid to tourism. Lack of facilities made travel in Iran a rugged experience. The Pahlavi government began paving highways and constructing hotels, and the number of tourists increased steadily in the years 1964–78. However, the political turmoil of 1978, which led to the overthrow of the monarchy, practically destroyed the tourist industry. The Islamic regime subsequently discouraged tourism from non-Muslim countries in an effort to exclude Western influences, and the services that depended on tourism collapsed as a result. In spite of government attempts to promote Iran as a tourist destination, services related to tourism remain a small sector of the economy.

LABOUR AND TAXATION

Although Iranian workers have, in theory, a right to form labour unions, there is, in actuality, no union system in the country. Workers are represented ostensibly by the Workers' House, a state-sponsored institution that nevertheless attempts to challenge some state policies. Guild unions operate locally in most areas but are limited largely to issuing credentials and licenses. The right of workers to strike is generally not respected by the state, and since 1979 strikes have often been met by police action.

Roughly one-fourth of Iran's labour force is engaged in manufacturing and construction. Another one-fifth is engaged in agriculture, and the remainder are divided almost evenly between occupations in services, transportation and communication, and finance. Women are allowed to work outside the home but face restrictions in a number of occupations, and the number of women in the workforce is relatively small in light of their level of education. Some of the numerous refugees in the country are allowed to work but, with the exception of a highly skilled minority, are generally restricted to low-wage, manual labour positions in construction and agriculture.

The minimum age for workers in Iran is 15 years, but large sectors of the economy (including small businesses, agricultural concerns, and family-owned enterprises) are exempted. The workweek is six days (48 hours), and the day of rest—as in many Muslim countries—is on Friday.

Income from petroleum and natural gas exports typically provides the largest share of government revenue, although this varies with the fluctuations in world petroleum markets. Taxes include those on corporations and import duties. In addition to these mandatory taxes, Islamic taxes are collected on a voluntary basis. These include an individual's income tax (Arabic: *khums*, "one-fifth"); an alms-tax (*zakāt*), which has a variable rate and benefits charitable causes; and a land tax (*kharāj*), the rate of which is based on the principle of one-tenth (*'ūshr*) of the value of crops, unless the land is tax-exempt.

TRANSPORTATION AND TELECOMMUNICATIONS

Iran's large centres of population are widely scattered, and transportation is made difficult by mountainous and desert terrain. Low funding and poor maintenance long reduced the efficiency of the highways. Nevertheless, motor vehicles—buses and trucks in particular—are the most important means of transportation for both passengers and goods. Since the early 1990s the Iranian government has allocated considerable resources to road construction and repair, and about half the roads are now paved.

The principal line of the state-owned railway system runs between the Caspian Sea and the Persian Gulf, with spur lines to many provincial capitals. In 1971 the railway was linked through Turkey with the European system; the link stimulated trade and tourism appreciably, undercutting airfares and significantly reducing sea transportation time. The Iranian portion of a line eastward to Singapore was completed as far as Mashhad by 1971. There is also a connection with railroads in Transcaucasia via Jolfā in the northwest, and a line completed in 1991 between Bafq

Citizens and state officials gather to acknowledge the inauguration of the Mashhad-Bafq Railway in 2005. The linkage of Iranian railways with the European system through Turkey has encouraged the development of trade and promoted tourism. © AP Images

and Bandar ʿAbbās links Iran's rail system to Central Asia; thus, Iran has begun to promote itself as a cost-efficient transport outlet for the states in that region.

The Kārūn is the only navigable river and is used to transport passengers and cargo. Lake Urmia has regular passenger and cargo ferry service between the port of Sharafkhāneh in the northeast and Golmānkhāneh in the southwest. Iran is served by five major ports on the Persian Gulf, the largest being Bandar ʿAbbās. Oil terminals at Ābādān and Khārk Island, destroyed or damaged in the war with Iraq, have since been rebuilt, as have port facilities at Khorramshahr and Bandar-e Khomeynī. Iran has expanded its facilities at the port of Būshehr and built a new port at Chāh Bahār (Bandar Beheshtī) on the Gulf of Oman. Caspian seaports, including Bandar-e Anzalī (formerly Bandar-e Pahlavī) and Bandar-e Torkaman (formerly Bandar-e Shāh), are primarily used for trade with nations to the north.

Bandar ʿAbbās

Bandar ʿAbbās (Persian: "Port of ʿAbbās"), a port city on the Strait of Hormuz, is the main maritime outlet for much of southern Iran. It lies on the northern shore of Hormuz Bay opposite the islands of Qeshm, Lārak, and Hormuz. The inhabitants are mainly Arabs and Africans. The summer climate is oppressively hot and humid, and many inhabitants then move to cooler places; however, winter is pleasant.

Bandar ʿAbbās was established in 1623 by Shah ʿAbbās I to replace the city of Hormuz, which had been captured by the Portuguese about 1514. During the 17th century it was the main port of Persia, but it lost this status in the 18th century to the rival Bandar-e Būshehr ("Port of Būshehr"). From about 1793 Bandar ʿAbbās was under lease to the rulers of Muscat, but in 1868 Iran canceled the contract and resumed direct control.

The port's imports consist mainly of manufactured goods; its exports include Kermān rugs, petroleum products, and agricultural produce. The town has a cotton mill, a fish cannery, and an oil refinery (opened in 1991). A natural gas refinery was under construction in the mid-1990s. The roadstead is shallow and badly sheltered, and vessels must sometimes lie 4 miles (6.5 km) out. In spite of the poor quality of its port facilities, the town boomed during the Iran-Iraq War of the 1980s when Iran's more westerly ports were threatened. A new harbour and shipbuilding yard were under construction in the late 20th century west of the existing port, and a major rail link was completed in 1995.

The state-owned airline, Iran Air, serves the major cities and provincial capitals. Some major European, Asian, and African airlines also serve Iran. Tehrān, Ābādān, Eṣfahān, Shīrāz, and Bandar ʿAbbās have international airports.

Telecommunications media in Iran are state-owned, and during the 1990s the state committed significant resources to developing and expanding its communications infrastructure. During that time the number of telephones nearly doubled. Telephone service was increased to rural areas, and by 2000 virtually every Iranian had access to service. Cellular telephone use, once limited, increased dramatically in the first decade of the 21st century, and Internet connectivity, which has provided Iranians—and especially Iranian youth—with a window to the outside world and accelerated interest in global culture, has expanded greatly as well. The scope of cellular-telephone and Internet use was demonstrated during the disputed 2009 presidential election and its attendant unrest, when protesters used electronic means to organize themselves and ensure that coverage of the events was available abroad.

Government and Society

Iran's 1979 constitution established the country as an Islamic republic and put into place a mixed system of government, in which the executive, parliament, and judiciary are overseen by several bodies dominated by the clergy. At the head of both the state and oversight institutions is the leader, or *rahbar*, a ranking cleric whose duties and authority are those usually equated with a head of state.

CHAPTER 4

VELĀYAT-E FAQĪH

The justification for Iran's mixed system of government can be found in the concept of *velāyat-e faqīh*, as expounded by Ayatollah Ruhollah Khomeini, the first leader of postrevolutionary Iran. Khomeini's method gives political leadership—in the absence of the divinely inspired imam—to the *faqīh*, or jurist in Islamic canon law, whose characteristics best qualify him to lead the community. Khomeini, the leader of the revolution (*rahbar-e enqelāb*), was widely believed to be such a man, and through his authority the position of leader was enshrined in the Iranian constitution. The Assembly of Experts (Majles-e Khobregān), an institution composed of ulama, chooses the leader from among qualified Shīʿite clergy on the basis of the candidate's personal piety, expertise in Islamic law, and political acumen.

The powers of the leader are extensive. He appoints the senior officers of the military and Revolutionary Guards (Pāsdārān-e Enqelāb), as well as the clerical members of the Council of Guardians (Shūrā-ye Negahbān) and members of the judiciary. The leader is also exclusively responsible for declarations of war and is the commander in chief of Iran's armed forces. Most important, the leader sets the general direction of the country's policy. There are no limits on the leader's term in office, but the Assembly of Experts may remove the leader from office if they find that he is unable to execute his duties.

Upon the death of Khomeini in June 1989, the Assembly of Experts elected Ayatollah Ali Khamenei as his successor, an unexpected move because of Khamenei's relatively low clerical status at the time of his nomination as leader. He was eventually accepted by Iranians as an ayatollah, however, through the urging of senior clerics—a unique event in Shīʿite Islam—and was elevated to the position of *rahbar* because of his political acumen.

The Presidency

The president, who is elected by universal adult suffrage, heads the executive branch and must be a native-born Iranian Shīʿite. This post was largely ceremonial until July 1989, when a national referendum approved a constitutional amendment that abolished the post of prime minister and vested greater authority in the president.

The president selects the Council of Ministers for approval by the legislature, appoints a portion of the members of the Committee to Determine the Expediency of the Islamic Order, and serves as chairman of the Supreme Council for National Security, which oversees the country's defense. The president and his ministers are responsible for the day-to-day administration of the government and the implementation of laws enacted by the legislature. In addition, the president oversees a wide range of government offices and organizations.

Ali Akbar Hashemi Rafsanjani, shown voting during the 2000 elections, was the first Iranian president to benefit from a constitutional amendment granting greater authority to the country's highest office. Scott Peterson/ Getty Images

LOCAL GOVERNMENT

Iran's *ostānhā* (provinces) are subdivided into *shahrestānhā* (counties), *bakhshhā* (districts), and *dehestānhā* (townships). The minister of the interior appoints the governors-general (for provinces) and governors (for counties). At each level there is a council, and the Supreme Council of Provinces is formed from representatives of the provincial councils. The ministry of the interior appoints each city's mayor, but city councilmen are locally elected. Villages are administered by a village master advised by elders.

Deliberative Bodies

The unicameral legislature is the Islamic Consultative Assembly (Majles-e Shūrā-ye Eslāmī), known simply as the Majles. Deputies are elected directly for four-year terms by universal adult suffrage, and recognized religious and ethnic minorities have token representation in the legislature. The Majles enacts all legislation and, under extraordinary circumstances, may impeach the president with a two-thirds majority vote.

The Council of Guardians is a body of jurists—half its members specialists in Islamic canon law appointed by the leader and the other half civil jurists nominated by the Supreme Judicial Council and appointed by the Majles—that acts in many ways as an upper legislative house. The council reviews all legislation passed by the Majles to determine its constitutionality. If a majority of the council does not find a piece of legislation in compliance with the constitution or if a majority of the council's Islamic canon lawyers find the document to be contrary to the standards of Islamic law, then the council may strike it down or return it with revisions to the Majles for reconsideration. In addition, the council supervises elections, and all candidates standing for election—even for the presidency—must meet with its prior approval.

In 1988 Khomeini ordered the formation of the Committee to Determine the Expediency of the Islamic Order—consisting of several members from the Council of Guardians and several members appointed by the president—to arbitrate disagreements between the Majles and the Council of Guardians. The Assembly of Experts, a body of clerics, was originally formed to draft the 1979 constitution. Since that time its sole function has been to select a new leader in the event of the death or incapacitation of the incumbent. If a suitable candidate is not found, the assembly may appoint a governing council of three to five members in the leader's stead.

JUSTICE

The judiciary consists of a Supreme Court, a Supreme Judicial Council, and lower courts. The chief justice and the prosecutor general must be specialists in Shīʿite canon law who have attained the status of *mujtahid*. Under the 1979 constitution all judges must base their decisions on the Sharīʿah (Islamic law). In 1982 the Supreme Court struck down any portion of the law codes of the deposed monarchy that did not conform with the Sharīʿah. In 1983 the Majles revised the penal code and instituted a system that embraced the form and content of Islamic law. This code implemented a series of traditional punishments, including retributions (Arabic: *qiṣāṣ*) for murder and other violent crimes—wherein the nearest relative of a murdered party may, if the court approves, take the life of the killer. Violent corporal punishments, including execution, are now the required form of chastisement for a wide range of crimes, ranging from adultery to alcohol consumption. With the number of clergy within the judiciary growing since the revolution, the state in 1987 implemented a special court outside of the regular judiciary to try members of the clergy accused of crimes.

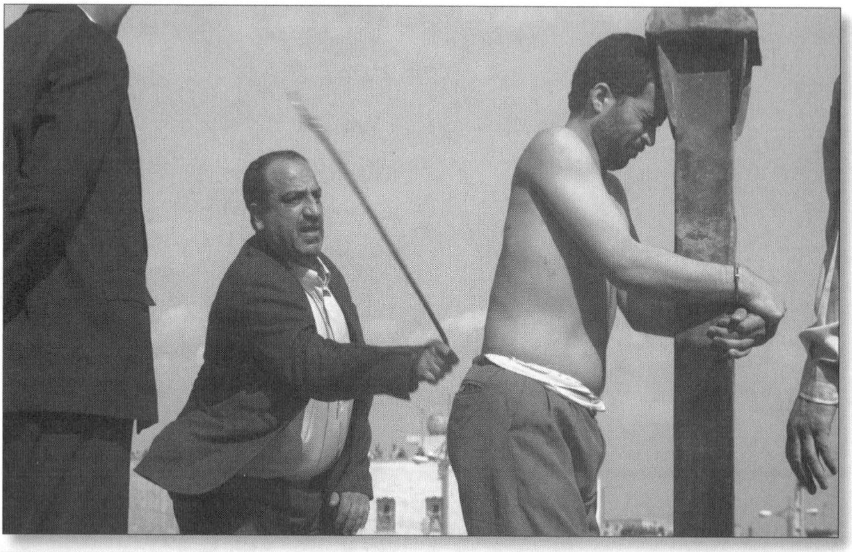

Flogging is one form of justice exacted by Iranian courts. Public lashings, stonings, and hangings are part of a penal code in Iran that embraces punishments prescribed by Islamic law. Behrouz Mehri/AFP/Getty Images

POLITICAL PROCESS

Under the constitution, elections are to be held at least every four years, supervised by the Council of Guardians. Suffrage is universal, and the minimum voting age is 16. All important matters are subject to referenda. At the outset of the revolution, the Islamic Republic Party was the ruling political party in Iran, but it subsequently proved to be too volatile, and Khomeini ordered it disbanded in 1987. The Muslim People's Republic Party, which once claimed more than three million members, and its leader, Ayatollah Mohammad Kazem Shariat-Madari, opposed many of Khomeini's reforms and the ruling party's tactics in the early period of the Islamic republic, but in 1981 it, too, was ordered to dissolve. The government has likewise outlawed several parties—including the Tūdeh ("Masses") Party, the Mojāhedīn-e Khalq ("Holy Warriors for the People") Party, and the Democratic Party of Iranian Kurdistan—although it permits parties that demonstrate what it considers to be a "commitment to the Islamic system."

SECURITY

Under the monarchy, Iran had one of the largest armed forces in the world, but it quickly dissolved with the collapse of the monarchy. Reconstituted following the revolution, the Iranian military engaged in a protracted war with Iraq (1980–88) and has since maintained a formidable active and reserve component. Since the mid-1980s Iran has sought to establish programs to develop weapons of mass destruction, including nuclear, biological, and chemical weapons (Iran used the latter in its war with Iraq), and by the late 1990s it had achieved some success in the domestic production of medium- and intermediate-range

Members of Iran's Revolutionary Guard pray in Tehran. Second only to the country's army when it comes to military might, the Guard is charged mainly with upholding Islamic law and tradition. Scott Peterson/Getty Images

missiles—effective from 300 to 600 miles (480 to 965 km) and from 600 to 3,300 miles (965 to 5,310 km) away, respectively. Outside observers, particularly those within the United States, have contended that Iran's fledgling nuclear energy industry is in fact the seedbed for a nuclear weapons program.

Iran's military obtains much of its manpower from conscription, and males are required to serve 21 months of military service. The army is the largest branch of Iran's military, followed by the Revolutionary Guards. This body, organized in the republic's early days, is the country's most effective military force and consists of the most politically dependable and religiously devout personnel. Any security forces that are involved in external war or in armed internal conflict are either accompanied or led by elements of the Revolutionary Guards. Iran has only a small air force and navy. A national police force is responsible for law enforcement in the cities, and a gendarmerie oversees rural areas. Both are under the direction of the Ministry of Interior.

HEALTH AND WELFARE

Health conditions appreciably improved after World War II through the combined efforts of the government, international agencies, and philanthropic endeavour. By 1964 smallpox had been eradicated, plague had disappeared, and malaria had been practically wiped out. Cholera, believed to have been controlled, broke out in 1970 and again in 1981 but was speedily checked. Health facilities, nevertheless, are far from adequate. There is a severe shortage, especially in rural areas, of doctors, nurses, and medical supplies.

Public hospitals provide free treatment for the poor. These are supplemented by private institutions, but all

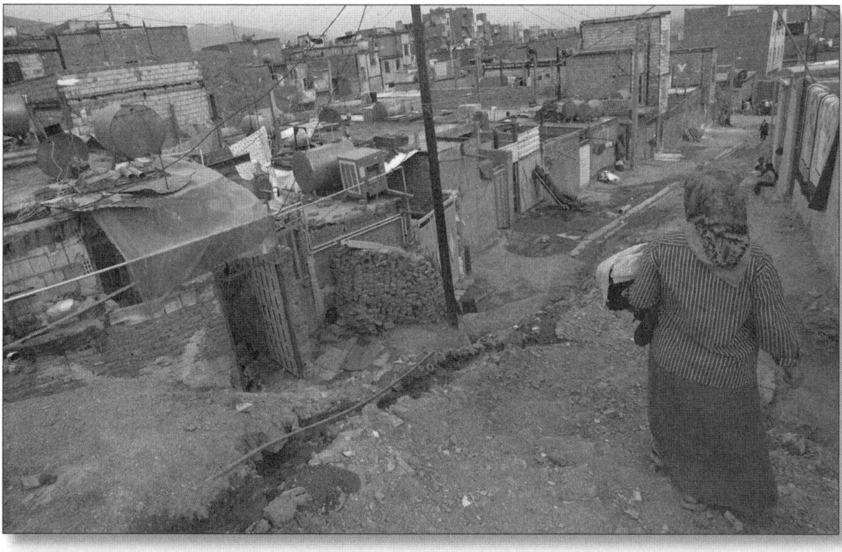

An Iranian woman walks in a poor neighbourhood on the outskirts of Tehrān. For segments of the population, including refugees and the urban poor, living conditions are harsh. Behrouz Mehri/AFP/Getty Images

are inadequate. All health services are supervised by the Ministry of Health, Treatment, and Medical Education, the branch offices of which are headed by certified physicians. Welfare is administered by the Ministry of State for Welfare, Foundation of the Oppressed (Bonyād-e Mostaẕʻafān), and the Martyr Foundation (Bonyād-e Shahīd), the latter being particularly concerned with families of war casualties.

HOUSING

The flow of population to the cities has created serious housing shortages, and it was only in the 1990s that the government began to address the housing crisis, largely by providing government credits for private sector development. However, most of the country's energies have been devoted to urban developments—most of those in the larger cities, particularly Tehrān—and habitation in rural areas remains austere. In major cities, purified water is piped into the houses, while small towns and villages rely on wells, *qanāts* (underground canals), springs, or rivers. Central heating is not common, except for modern buildings in major cities, and portable kerosene heaters, iron stoves using wood and coal, and charcoal braziers are common sources of heat. Living conditions remain especially harsh among the urban poor and the enormous refugee population.

EDUCATION

Education is compulsory between the ages of 6 and 11. Roughly nine-tenths of men and four-fifths of women are literate. Primary education is followed by a three-year guidance cycle, which assesses students' aptitudes and determines whether they will enter an academic, scientific, or vocational program during high school. Policy changes initiated since the revolution eliminated coeducational schools and required all schools and universities to promote Islamic values. The latter is a reaction to the strong current of Western secularism that permeated higher education under the monarchy. Adherence to the prevalent political dogma has long been an important factor for students and faculty who wish to succeed in Iranian universities. In fact, acceptance to universities in Iran is largely based on a candidate's personal piety, either real or perceived.

The University of Tehrān was founded in 1934, and several more universities, teachers' colleges, and technical schools have been established since then. Iran's institutes of higher learning suffered after the revolution,

Students studying inside the Tehrān University library. Post-revolution enrollment is down in Iranian institutions of higher learning, yet more women are attending classes than ever before. Barry Iverson/Time & Life Pictures/ Getty Images

however, when tens of thousands of professors and instructors either fled the country or were dismissed because of their secularism or association with the monarchy. Iran's universities have remained understaffed, and thus student enrollment has dropped in a country that greatly esteems higher education. The shortage of skilled teachers has led the government to encourage students to study abroad, in an effort to improve the quality and quantity of advanced degree holders and faculty. While overall enrollment numbers have fallen, the rate of women's admission at the university level has climbed dramatically, and by 2000 more than half of incoming students were women.

The public school system is controlled by the Ministry of Education and Training. Universities are under the supervision of the Ministry of Higher Education and Culture, and medical schools are under the Ministry of Health, Treatment, and Medical Education.

CHAPTER 5

Cultural Life

Few countries enjoy such a long cultural heritage as does Iran, and few people are so aware of and articulate about their deep cultural tradition as are the Iranians. Iran, or Persia, as a historical entity, dates to the time of the Achaemenids (about 2,500 years ago), and, in spite of political, religious, and historic changes, Iranians maintain a deep connection to their past. Although daily life in modern Iran is closely interwoven with Shīʿite Islam, the country's art, literature, and architecture are an ever-present reminder of its deep national tradition and of a broader literary culture that during the premodern period spread throughout the Middle East and South Asia. Much of Iran's modern history can be attributed to the essential tension that existed between the Shīʿite piety promoted by Iran's clergy and the Persian cultural legacy—in which religion played a subordinate role—proffered by the Pahlavi monarchy.

In spite of the predominance of Persian culture, Iran remains a multiethnic state, and the country's Armenian, Azerbaijanian, Kurdish, and smaller ethnic minorities each have their own literary and historical traditions dating back many centuries, even—in the case of the Armenians—to the pre-Christian era. These groups frequently maintain close connections with the larger cultural life of their kindred outside Iran.

DAILY LIFE AND SOCIAL CUSTOMS

The narrative of martyrdom has been an essential component of Shīʿite culture, which can be traced to the massacre in 680 of the third imam, al-Ḥusayn ibn ʿAlī, along with his close family and followers at the Battle of Karbalāʾ by the troops of the Ummayad caliph, Yazīd, during al-Ḥusayn's failed attempt to restore his family line to political power. As a minority in the Islamic community, Shīʿites faced much persecution and, according to Shīʿite doctrine, offered up many martyrs over the centuries because of their belief in the right of the line of ʿAlī to political rule and religious leadership. Each year on the anniversary of the massacre, Shīʿites commemorate the Karbalāʾ tragedy during the holiday of ʿĀshūrāʾ through the *taʿziyyah* (passion play) and through rituals of self-flagellation with bare hands and, sometimes, with chains and blades. These acts of mourning continue throughout the year in the practice of the *rawẕeh khānī*, a ritual of mourning in which a storyteller, the *rawẕeh khān*, incites the assembled—who are frequently gathered at a special place of mourning called a *ḥosayniyyeh*—to tears by tales of the death of al-Ḥusayn.

The commemoration of Karbalāʾ has permeated all of Persian culture and finds expression in poetry, music, and the solemn Shīʿite view of the world. No religious ceremony is complete without a reference to Karbalāʾ, and no month passes without at least one day of mourning. None of the efforts of the monarchy, such as the annual festivals of art and the encouragement of musicians and native crafts, succeeded in changing this basic attitude; public displays of laughter and joy remain undesirable, even sinful, in some circles.

Iranians do celebrate several festive occasions. In addition to the two *ʿīd*s (Arabic: "holidays")—practiced by Sunnis and Shīʿites alike—the most important holidays are Nōrūz, the Persian New Year, and the birthday of the 12th imam, whose second coming the Shīʿites expect in the end of days. The Nōrūz celebration begins on the last Wednesday of the old year, is followed by a weeklong holiday, and continues until the 13th day of the new year, which is a day for picnicking in the countryside. On the

12th imam's birthday, cities sparkle with lights, and the bazaars are decorated and teem with shoppers.

Persian cuisine, although strongly influenced by the culinary traditions of the Arab world and the subcontinent, is largely a product of the geography and domestic food products of Iran. Rice is a dietary staple, and meat—mostly lamb—plays a part in virtually every meal. Vegetables are central to the Iranian diet, with onions an ingredient of virtually every dish. Herding has long been a traditional part of the economy, and dairy products—milk, cheese, and particularly yogurt—are common ingredients in Persian dishes. Traditional Persian cuisine tends to favour subtle flavours and relatively simple preparations such as *khūresh* (stew) and kabobs. Saffron is the most distinctive spice used, but many other flavourings—including lime, mint, turmeric, and rosewater—are common, as are pomegranates and walnuts.

Al-Ḥusayn ibn ʿAlī

(b. January 626, Medina, Arabia [now in Saudi Arabia]—d. Oct. 10, 680, Karbalāʾ, Iraq)

Al-Ḥusayn ibn ʿAlī was the grandson of the Prophet Muhammad and son of ʿAlī (the fourth Islamic caliph) and Fāṭimah, daughter of Muhammad. A Shīʿite Muslim hero, he is revered by Shīʿites as the third imam (after ʿAlī and al-Ḥusayn's older brother, Ḥasan).

After the assassination of their father, ʿAlī, Ḥasan and al-Ḥusayn acquiesced to the rule of the first Umayyad caliph, Muʿāwiyah, from whom they received pensions. Al-Ḥusayn, however, refused to recognize the legitimacy of Muʿāwiyah's son and successor, Yazīd (April 680). Al-Ḥusayn was then invited by the townsmen of Kūfah, a city with a Shīʿite majority, to come there and raise the standard of revolt against the Umayyads. After receiving some favourable indications, al-Ḥusayn set out for Kūfah with a small band of relatives and followers. According to traditional accounts, he met the poet al-Farazdaq on the way and was told that the hearts of the Iraqis were for him, but their swords were for the Umayyads. The governor of Iraq, on behalf of the caliph, sent 4,000 men to arrest al-Ḥusayn and his small band. They trapped al-Ḥusayn near the banks of the Euphrates River (October 680). When al-Ḥusayn refused to surrender, he and his escort were slain, and al-Ḥusayn's head was sent to Yazīd in Damascus.

In remembrance of the martyrdom of al-Ḥusayn, Shīʿite Muslims observe the first 10 days of Muḥarram (the date of the battle according to the Islamic calendar) as days of lamentation. Revenge for al-Ḥusayn's death was turned into a rallying cry that helped undermine the Umayyad caliphate and gave impetus to the rise of a powerful Shīʿite movement.

The details of al-Ḥusayn's life are obscured by the legends that grew up surrounding his martyrdom, but his final acts appear to have been inspired by a definite ideology—to found a regime that would reinstate a "true" Islamic polity as opposed to what he considered the unjust rule of the Umayyads.

THE ARTS

Iran lays claim to a rich artistic heritage. In addition to traditional arts and crafts, including metalwork, carpet making, and textile weaving, Iran has also given rise to a range of literary and cinematic achievements. Iran's splendid historical heritage is still evident in numerous archaeological remains, some of which have been officially recognized and protected as sites of extraordinary historical and cultural worth.

Crafts

Carpet looms dot the country. Each locality prides itself on a special design and quality of carpet that bears its name, such as Kāshān, Kermān, Khorāsān, Eṣfahān, Shīrāz, Tabrīz, and Qom. Carpets are used locally and are exported. The handwoven-cloth industry has survived stiff competition from modern textile mills. Weavers produce velvets, printed cottons, wool brocades, shawls, and cloth shoes. Felt is made in the south, and sheepskin is embroidered in the northeast.

A wide range of articles, both utilitarian and decorative, are made of various metals. The best-known centres are Tehrān (gold); Shīrāz, Eṣfahān, and Zanjān (silver); and Kāshān and Eṣfahān (copper). Khorāsān is known for its turquoise working and the Persian Gulf region for its natural pearls. The craft techniques are as divergent as the products themselves. Articles may be cast, beaten, wrought, pierced, or drawn (stretched out). The most widespread techniques for ornamentation are engraving, embossing, chiseling, damascening, encrustation, or gilding.

Numerous decorative articles in wood are produced for both the domestic and export markets in Eṣfahān, Shīrāz, and Tehrān (inlay) and in Rasht, Orūmiyyeh (formerly called Reẕā'iyyeh), and Sanandaj (carved and pierced wood). Machine-made ceramic tiles are manufactured in Tehrān, but handmade tiles and mosaics, known for their rich designs and beautiful colours, also continue to be produced.

Stone and clay are also used for the production of a wide range of household utensils, trays, dishes, and vases. Mashhad is the centre of the stone industry. Potteries are widely scattered throughout the country, Hamadān being the largest centre.

Architecture

Iran's ancient culture has a deep architectural tradition. The Elamite, Achaemenian, Hellenistic, and other pre-Islamic dynasties left striking stone testaments to their greatness, such as Choghā Zanbil and Persepolis—both of which were designated UNESCO World Heritage

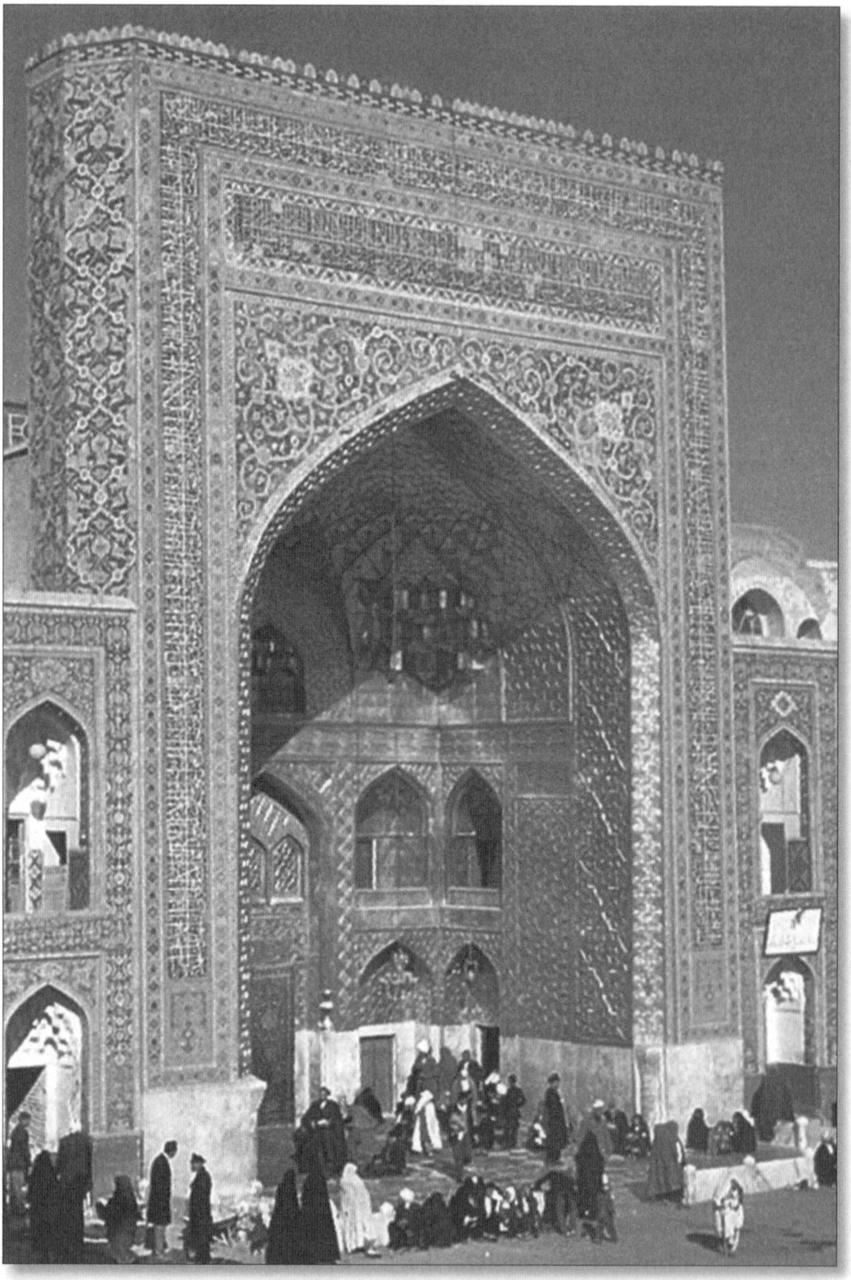

Shrine of imam ʿAlī al-Riḍā, Mashhad, Iran. Fred J. Maroon/Photo Researchers

sites in 1979. Three monastic ensembles central to the Armenian Christian faith were collectively recognized as a World Heritage site in 2008; their architecture represents a confluence of Byzantine, Persian, and Armenian cultures.

From the Islamic period the architectural achievements of the Seljuq, Il-Khanid, and Ṣafavid dynasties are particularly noteworthy. During that time Iranian cities such as Neyshābūr, Eṣfahān, and Shīrāz came to be among the great cities of the Islamic world, and their many mosques, madrasahs, shrines, and palaces formed an architectural

Dome of the Shrine of Fāṭimah, Qom, Iran. Kurt Scholz/Shostal Associates

tradition that was distinctly Iranian within the larger Islamic milieu.

Under the Pahlavi monarchy, two architectural trends developed—an imitation of Western styles, which had little relevance to the country's climate and landscape, and an attempt to revive indigenous designs. The National Council for Iranian Architecture, founded in 1967, discouraged blind imitation of the West and promoted the use

The Āzādī ("Freedom") tower, Tehrān. Photos.com/Jupiterimages

of more traditional Iranian styles that were modified to serve modern needs. Perhaps the most striking example of the Pahlavi architectural program is the Shāhyād (Persian: "Shah's Monument") tower—renamed the Āzādī ("Freedom") tower after the Islamic revolution—which was completed in Tehrān in 1971 to commemorate the 2,500th anniversary of the founding of the Achaemenian dynasty.

Choghā Zanbīl

Choghā Zanbīl—also spelled Tchoghā Zanbīl or Choga Zambil—is a ruined palace and temple complex of the ancient Elamite city of Dur Untashi (Dur Untash), near Susa in the Khūzestān region of southwestern Iran. The complex consists of a magnificent ziggurat (the largest structure of its kind in Iran), temples, and three palaces. The site was added to UNESCO's World Heritage List in 1979.

Built about 1250 BCE under the direction of the Elamite ruler Untash-Gal during the Middle Elamite period (*c.* 1500–*c.* 1000 BCE), the complex was dedicated to Inshushinak (Insusinak), the bull-god of Susa. Its irregularly shaped outer wall extends approximately 3,900 by 2,600 feet (1,200 by 800 metres) around the inner sanctum and 13 temple buildings, of which only four are well conserved. The square base of the ziggurat, 344 feet (105 metres) on each side, was built principally of brick and cement. It now stands 80 feet (24 metres) high, less than half its estimated original height. Its ornate facade was once covered in glazed blue and green terracotta, and its interior was decorated in glass and ivory mosaics. At

Ziggurat at Choghā Zanbīl near Susa, Iran. Robert Harding Picture Library/Sybil Sassoon

the apex of the building stood a temple from which Inshushinak was believed to ascend to the heavens every night. The complex was still unfinished, however (as evidenced by thousands of stacked bricks at the site), by about 640 BCE, when Choghā Zanbīl was attacked, looted, and heavily damaged by the forces of the Assyrian king Ashurbanipal. Afterward it fell into ruin.

Choghā Zanbīl is a local name meaning "large basket-shaped hill." It was sighted in 1935 by prospectors of the Anglo-Iranian Oil Company who were surveying the region by airplane. Initial studies were performed by French archaeologists in the late 1930s. From 1946 to 1962, excavations were carried out by the archaeologist Roman Ghirshman. Several bull sculptures of Inshushinak were found within the complex, which served the royal families of Elam as a place both of worship and of interment. In addition, a variety of small artifacts were recovered, including a collection of Middle Elamite cylinder seals. A building on the grounds contains five vaulted underground tombs, within four of which are cremated remains, and there is one uncremated corpse. The Elamites traditionally buried their dead, and the reason for the cremation is unknown.

Heavy precipitation has had a harmful effect on the mud-brick outer walls and temples of the complex, in spite of the application of protective coverings. In the mid-1990s, it was noted that the brick walls of the ziggurat had shifted slightly, raising concerns about future structural damage.

Visual Arts

Islamic culture never developed strong indigenous schools of visual arts, perhaps because of the religion's rejection of any form of idolatry or graphic depiction of any form. A significant exception to this rule was the development in Iran of highly refined miniature painting—noteworthy were the Jalāyirid, Shīrāz, and Eṣfahān schools. Persian miniature, however, largely died out by the late Ṣafavid period (late 18th century). This did not prevent Iranian artists from working in other media, such as calligraphy, illumination, weaving, ceramics, and metalwork. Western classical painting and sculpture were introduced in the late 19th century and were adapted to Iranian themes. The trend toward Islamization after the Islamic revolution restricted visual arts, but this medium nevertheless continued to develop through exhibits and, more recently, through access to the Internet.

Music

For centuries Islamic injunctions inhibited the development of formal musical disciplines, but folk songs and ancient Persian classical music were preserved through oral transmission from generation to generation. It was not until the 20th century that a music conservatory was founded in Tehrān and that Western techniques were used to record traditional melodies and encourage new compositions. This trend was reversed, however, in 1979, when the former restrictions on the study and practice of music were restored. Although officially forbidden—even after the liberal reforms of the late 1990s—Western pop music is fashionable among Iranian youth, and there is a thriving trade in musical cassette tapes and compact discs. Iranian pop groups also occasionally perform, though often under threat of punishment. In 2000, Iranian authorities permitted Googoosh, the most popular Iranian singer of the prerevolutionary era, to resume her career—albeit from abroad—after 21 years of forced silence.

Googoosh

(b. 1950, Tehrān, Iran)

Googoosh, whose original name was Faegheh Atashin, is an Iranian singer and actress who was one of Iran's most popular and enduring entertainers in spite of being banned from performing for some 20 years following the Islamic Revolution (1978–79).

Nicknamed "Googoosh" from birth, she began singing and acting at a young age, performing with her father, an entertainer, when she was a toddler and making her first film at age seven. She later appeared in such movies as *Partgahe makhouf* (1963; *Cliff of Fear*), *Sheitune bala* (1965; *The Naughty One*), and *Panjereh* (1970; *The Window*). In the 1970s Googoosh was at the height of her film and music career and was widely emulated by Iranian women; in addition to listening to her music, they copied her clothing (miniskirts) and her short haircut (known as the "Googooshy"). In 1979, however, Iran was declared an Islamic republic, and a number of cultural restrictions were introduced; women were no longer allowed to sing in public, and pop music was banned. Although most Iranian performers chose to leave the country, Googoosh, who was visiting the United States at the time of the revolution, returned home. She was jailed briefly and thereafter led a reclusive life.

Bootleg recordings and videos remained readily available in Iran, however, and Googoosh continued to acquire fans. Following the election of Pres. Mohammad Khatami in 1997, many restrictions began to be lifted. Some women (Googoosh was not among them) were allowed to sing in public to all-female audiences, and, while distributing pop music was still officially illegal, possession of it was permitted. In 2000 Googoosh finally was granted a passport and allowed to leave the country for the first time since the revolution. That year she staged her first world tour, which began in Toronto, where she and her husband, Iranian film director Masud Kimiai, eventually settled. Googoosh's later recordings include *Zoroaster* (2000) and *Last News* (2004).

LITERATURE

Iranian culture is perhaps best known for its literature, which emerged in its current form in the 9th century. The great masters of the Persian language—Ferdowsī, Neẓāmī, Ḥāfeẓ, Jāmī, and Rūmī—continue to inspire Iranian authors in the modern era, although publication and distribution of many classical works—deemed licentious by conservative clerics—have been difficult.

Gardens at the tomb of the poet Hāfeẓ, Shīrāz, Iran. Paolo Koch/Photo Researchers

Persian literature was deeply influenced by Western literary and philosophical traditions in the 19th and 20th centuries yet remains a vibrant medium for Iranian culture. Whether in prose or in poetry, it also came to serve as a vehicle of cultural introspection, political dissent, and personal protest for such influential Iranian writers as Sadeq Hedayat, Jalal Al-e Ahmad, and Sadeq-e Chubak and such poets as Ahmad Shamlu and Forough Farrokhzad. Following the Islamic revolution of 1978–79, many Iranian writers went into exile, and much of the country's best Persian-language literature was thereafter written and published abroad. However, the postrevolutionary era also witnessed the birth of a new feminist literature by authors such as Shahrnoush Parsipour and Moniru Ravanipur.

Sadeq Hedayat

(b. Feb. 17, 1903, Tehrān, Iran—d. April 4, 1951, Paris, France)

Sadeq Hedayat was an Iranian author who introduced modernist techniques into Persian fiction. He is considered one of the greatest Iranian writers of the 20th century.

Born into a prominent aristocratic family, Hedayat was educated first in Tehrān and then studied dentistry and engineering in France and Belgium. After coming into contact with the leading intellectual figures of Europe, Hedayat abandoned his studies for literature.

He was intensely drawn to the works of Edgar Allan Poe, Guy de Maupassant, Rainer Maria Rilke, Franz Kafka, Anton Chekhov, and Fyodor Dostoyevsky. Hedayat translated into Persian many of Kafka's works, including *In the Penal Colony*, for which he wrote a revealing introduction called "Payām-e Kafka" ("Kafka's Message"). He returned to Iran in 1930 after four years and published his first book of short stories, *Zendeh be gūr* (1930; *Buried Alive*), and the first of three plays, *Parvīn dokhtar-e Sāsān* (*Parvin, Daughter of Sasan*). These he followed with the prose works *Sāyeh-ye Moghol* (1931; *Mongol Shadow*) and *Sē qaṭreh-khūn* (1932; *Three Drops of Blood*).

Hedayat was the central figure in Tehrān intellectual circles and belonged to the antimonarchical, anti-Islamic literary group known as the Four (which also included Buzurg 'Alavī). He began to develop a strong interest in Iranian folklore and published *Osāneh* (1931), a collection of popular songs, and *Nīrangestān* (1932). In these, Hedayat greatly enriched Persian prose and influenced younger writers through his use of folk expressions. He also wrote a number of critical articles and translated the works of leading European authors, Chekhov and Jean-Paul Sartre among them. He began to study history, beginning with the Sāsānian period (224–651) and the Pahlavi, or Middle Persian, language, and he used this study in later fiction. In 1936–37 he went to Bombay (now Mumbai) to live in the Parsi Zoroastrian community there, in order to further his knowledge of the ancient Iranian religion.

One of Hedayat's most famous novels, *Būf-e Kūr* (1937; *The Blind Owl*), is profoundly pessimistic and Kafkaesque. A deeply melancholy man, he lived with a vision of the absurdity of human existence and his inability to effect a change for the good in Iran. He withdrew from his friends and began to seek escape from his sense of futility in drugs and alcohol. In 1951, overwhelmed by despair, he left Tehrān and went to Paris, where he took his own life.

Among Hedayat's books published in English are *Haji Agha: Portrait of an Iranian Confidence Man* (1979), *Sadeq Hedayat: An Anthology* (1979; short stories), and *The Myth of Creation* (1998; drama).

Cinema

The most popular form of entertainment in Iran is the cinema, which is also an important medium for social and political commentary in a society that has had little tolerance for participatory democracy. After the Islamic revolution the government at first banned filmmaking but then gave directors financial support if they agreed to propagate Islamic values. However, the public showed little interest, and this period of ideology-driven filmmaking did not last. Soon films that dealt with the Iran-Iraq War or that reflected more tolerant expressions of Islamic values, including Sufi mysticism, gained ground.

The religious establishment, however, generally frowns upon the imitation of Western films among Iran's filmmakers but encourages adapting Western and Eastern classic stories and folktales, provided that they reflect contemporary Iranian concerns and not transgress Islamic restrictions imposed by the government. In the 1990s the fervour of the early revolutionary years was replaced by demands for political moderation and better relations with the West. Iran's film industry became one of the finest in the world, with festivals of Iranian films being held annually throughout the world. Directors Bahram Bayza'i, Abbas Kiarostami, Mohsen Makhmalbaf, and Dariyush Mehrju'i produced films that won numerous awards at international festivals, including Cannes (France) and Locarno (Switzerland), and a new generation of women film directors—among them Rakhshan Bani E'temad (*Blue Scarf*, 1995) and Tahmineh Milani (*Two Women*, 1999)—has also emerged.

Iran's filmmakers are celebrated for films that deal with the lives of children (*Bashu the Stranger*, 1989; *The White Balloon*, 1995; *Children of Heaven*, 1997), the concerns and issues of teenagers (*The Need*, 1991; *Sweet Agony*, 1999), the beauty of nature (*Gabbeh*, 1996), and social and psychological abuse in marriage, divorce, and polygyny (*Leila*, 1996; *Two Women*; *Red*, 1999).

CULTURAL INSTITUTIONS

Iran has few museums, and those that exist are of relatively recent origin. The two exceptions are the Golestān Palace Museum in Tehrān, which was opened in 1894, and the All Saviour's Cathedral Museum of Jolfā (Eṣfahān), which was built by the Armenian community in 1905. The only gallery devoted solely to art is the Tehrān Museum of Modern Art, opened in 1977. Other well-known museums include the National Museum of Iran (1937) and Negārestān (1975) in Tehrān and Pārs (1938) in Shīrāz.

Among the learned societies, all of which are located in Tehrān, the most important are the Ancient Iranian Cultural Society, the Iranian Mathematical Society, and the Iranian Society of Microbiology. There are also a number of research institutes, such as those devoted to cultural, scientific, archaeological, anthropological, and historical topics. In addition to libraries at the various universities, there are public and private libraries in Tehrān, Mashhad, Eṣfahān, and Shīrāz.

SPORTS AND RECREATION

Wrestling, horse racing, and bodybuilding are the traditional sports of the country. Team sports were introduced from the West in the 20th century, the most popular being rugby football and volleyball. Under the monarchy, modern sports were incorporated into the school curricula. Iran's Physical Education Organization was formed in 1934. Iranian athletes first participated in the Olympics Games in 1948. The country made its Winter Games debut in 1956. All of Iran's Olympic medals have come in weight-lifting and wrestling events.

Football (soccer) has become the most popular game in Iran—the country's team won the Asian championships in 1968, 1974, and 1976 and made its World Cup debut in 1978—but the Islamic revolution was a major setback for Iranian sports. The new government regarded the sports stadium as a rival to the mosque. Major teams were nationalized, and women were prevented from participating in many activities. In addition, the Iran-Iraq War left few resources to devote to sports. However, the enormous public support for sports, especially for football, could not be easily suppressed. Since the 1990s there has been a revival of athletics in Iran, including women's activities. Sports have become inextricably bound up with demands for political liberalization, and nearly every major event has become an occasion for massive public celebrations by young men and women expressing their desire for reform and for more amicable relations with the West.

MEDIA AND PUBLISHING

Daily newspapers and periodicals are published primarily in Tehrān and must be licensed under the press law of 1979.

The publication of any anti-Muslim sentiment is strictly forbidden. Iran's Ministry of Culture and Islamic Guidance operates the Islamic Republic News Agency (IRNA). Foreign correspondents are allowed into the country on special occasions. In spite of constitutional guarantees of freedom of the press, censorship by conservative elements within the government is widespread, particularly in the electronic media. Regardless, print media—newspapers, magazines, and journals—contributed greatly to the growth of political reform in Iran during the late 1990s. The most widely circulated newspapers include *Eṭṭelāʿāt* and *Kayhān*.

Radio and television broadcasting stations in Iran are operated by the government and reach the entire country, and some radio broadcasts have international reception. The government made possession of satellite reception equipment illegal in 1995, but the ban has been irregularly enforced, and many Iranians have continued to receive television broadcasts—including Persian-language programs—from abroad. Programs are broadcast in Persian and some foreign languages, as well as in local languages and dialects. Though basic literacy increased substantially in the years following the revolution, audio-visual media have remained much more effective than print material for disseminating information, especially in rural areas.

History

Chapter 6

The territory that comprises the modern state of Iran has a lengthy history. The region was known for centuries—especially in the West—as Persia, to designate those regions where Persian language and culture predominated. (The term Persia more correctly refers to a region of southern Iran formerly known as Persis, alternatively as Pārs or Parsa, modern Fārs. Parsa was the name of an Indo-European nomadic people who migrated into the region about 1000 BCE.)

The country's roots as a distinctive culture and society date to the Achaemenian period, which began in 550 BCE; throughout its history the region has been influenced by waves of indigenous and foreign conquerors and immigrants, including the Hellenistic Seleucids and native Parthians and Sāsānids. The Arab invasion of Iran in the 7th century made a break with the past that affected not only Iran but all of western Asia and resulted in the assimilation of peoples who shaped and vitalized Muslim culture.

The Advent of Islam (640–829)

The Prophet Muhammad had made Medina, his adopted city, and Mecca, his birthplace, centres of an Arabian movement that Muslim Arabs developed into a world movement through the conquest of Iranian and Byzantine territories. Neither Sāsānian Iran nor the Byzantine Empire had been unfamiliar to those Arabs who were the former's Lakhmid and the latter's Ghassānid vassals, the frontier guardians of the two empires against fellow Arabs who roamed deeper in the Arabian Desert. Also, Meccan and Medinese Arabs had established commercial connections with the Byzantines and Sāsānids. The immunity of Mecca's ancient sanctuary, the Ka'bah, against outlawry and outrage had promoted this city's commercial importance. The Ka'bah was cleansed of idols by Muhammad, who had himself once been engaged in commerce. He made it the sanctuary of a monotheistic faith whose sacred writings were filled with the injunctions and prohibitions needed by a business community for secure and stable trading.

Arab tribalism beyond urban fringes was less easily broken than idols. It was embedded in the desert sparsity that led to warfare and carefully counting a tribe's male offspring. After Mecca and Medina had become Muslim, it was

A tile depicting Mecca, including the Ka'bah (black cube, centre), which is considered to be the most sacred spot on Earth by Muslims worldwide. The Bridgeman Art Library/Getty Images

essential that the Muslims win the desert Arabs' allegiance in order to secure the routes they depended on for trade and communication. In the process of doing this, wars over water holes, scanty pastures, men-at-arms, and camels were enlarged into international campaigns of expansion.

The vulnerability of Sāsānian Iran assisted the expansionist process. In 623 the Byzantine emperor Heraclius reversed Persian successes over Roman arms—namely, by capturing Jerusalem in 614 and winning at Chalcedon in 617. His victim, Khosrow Parvīz, died in 628 and left Iran prey to a succession of puppet rulers who were frequently deposed by a combination of nobles and Zoroastrian clergy. Thus, when Yazdegerd III, Iran's last Sāsānid and Zoroastrian sovereign, came to the throne in 632, the year of Muhammad's death, he inherited an empire weakened by Byzantine wars and internal dissension.

The former Arab vassals on the empire's southwestern border realized that their moment had arrived. But their raids into Sāsānian territory were quickly taken up by Muhammad's caliphs, or deputies, at Medina—Abū Bakr and 'Umar ibn al-Khaṭṭāb—to become a Muslim, pan-Arab attack on Iran.

An Arab victory at Al-Qādisiyyah in 636/637 was followed by the sack of the Sāsānian winter capital at Ctesiphon on the Tigris. The Battle of Nahāvand in 642 completed the Sāsānids' vanquishment. Yazdegerd fled to the empire's northeastern outpost, Merv, whose *marzbān*, or march lord, Mahūyeh, was soured by Yazdegerd's imperious and expensive demands. Mahūyeh turned against his emperor and defeated him with the help of Hephthalites from Bādghis. The Hephthalites, an independent border power, had troubled the Sāsānids since at least 590, when they had sided with Bahrām Chūbīn, Khosrow Parvīz's rebel general. A miller near Merv murdered the fugitive Yazdegerd for his purse.

The Sāsānids' end was ignominious, but it was not the end of Iran. Rather, it marked a new beginning. Within two centuries Iranian civilization was revived with a cultural amalgam, with patterns of art and thought, with attitudes and a sophistication that were indebted to its pre-Islamic Iranian heritage—a heritage changed but also stirred into fresh life by the Arab Muslim conquest.

Lakhmid Dynasty

The Lakhmids were a pre-Islamic Bedouin tribal dynasty that aided Sāsānian Iran in its struggle with the Byzantine Empire and fostered early Arabic poetry.

Centred at the Christian city of Al-Ḥīrah, near present-day Al-Kūfah in southern Iraq, the Lakhmid kingdom originated in the late 3rd century CE and developed essentially as an Iranian vassal state. Gaining a voice in Iranian affairs under King al-Mundhir I (ruled *c.* 418–462), who raised Bahrām V to the throne of the Sāsānian empire, the Lakhmids reached the height of their power in the 6th century, when al-Mundhir III (ruled 503–554) raided Byzantine Syria and challenged the pro-Byzantine Arab kingdom of Ghassān. His son ʿAmr ibn Hind (ruled 554–569) was patron of the pre-Islamic Arabic poetry of Ṭarafah and others associated with *Al-Muʿallaqāt* ("The Suspended Odes"). The dynasty became extinct with the death, in 602, of an-Nuʿmān III, who was a Nestorian Christian.

ABŪ MUSLIM'S REVOLUTION

Less time was needed before a new Islamic beginning: Abū Muslim's movement, which began in Khorāsān in 747 and was caused by Arab assimilation with Iranians in colonized regions. This revolution followed years of conspiracy directed from Medina and across to Khorāsān along the trade route that linked East Asia with Merv and thence with the West. Along the route, merchants with contacts in the Mesopotamian Arab garrison cities of Al-Kūfah, Wāsi, and Al-Başrah acted as intermediaries. Iranians who converted to Islam and became clients, or *al-mawālī*, of Arab patrons played direct and indirect parts in the revolutionary movement, which also involved Arabs who had become partners with Khorāsānian and Transoxanian Iranians in ventures in the great east-west trade and intercity trade of north-eastern Iran.

The revolution was, nevertheless, primarily an Arab Islamic movement that intended to supplant a militaristic, tyrannical central government—whose fiscal problems made it avid for revenue—by one more sympathetic to the needs of the merchants of eastern Islam. Abū Muslim, a revolutionary of unknown origin, was able to exploit the discontent of the merchant classes in Merv as well as that of the Arab and Iranian settlers. The object of attack was the Umayyad government in Damascus.

When Muhammad died in 632, his newly established community in Medina and Mecca needed a guiding counselor, an imam, to lead them in prayers and an *amīr al-mu'minīn*, a "commander of the faithful," to ensure proper application of the Prophet's divinely inspired precepts. As the Prophet, Muhammad could never be entirely succeeded, but it was accepted that men who had sufficient dignity and who had known him could fulfill the functions, as his caliphs (deputies) and imams. After Abū Bakr and 'Umar, 'Uthmān ibn 'Affān was chosen for this role.

By 'Uthmān's time, factionalism was growing among Arabs, partly the result of the jealousies and rivalries that accompanied the acquisition of new territories and partly the result of the competition between first arrivals there and those who followed. There was also uncertainty over the most desirable kind of imamate. One faction, the

Shīʿites, supported ʿAlī, Muhammad's cousin and the husband of the Prophet's favourite daughter, Fāṭimah, for the caliphate, since he had been an intimate of Muhammad and seemed more capable than the other candidates of expressing Muhammad's wisdom and virtue as the people's judge. The desire for such a successor points to disenchantment with ʿUthmān's attempt to strengthen the central government and impose demands on the colonies. His murder in 656 left his Umayyad relatives poised to avenge it, while ʿAlī was raised to the caliphate. A group of his supporters, the Khārijites, desired more freedom than ʿAlī was willing to grant, with a return to the simplest interpretation of the Prophet's revelation in the Qur'ān, along puritanical lines.

A Khārijite killed ʿAlī in 661. The Shīʿites thenceforth crystallized into the obverse position of the Khārijites, emphasizing ʿAlī's relationship to the Prophet as a means of making him and his descendants by Fāṭimah the sole legitimate heirs to the Prophet, some of whose spiritual power was even believed to have been transmitted to them. Centuries later this Shīʿism became the official Islamic sect of Iran. In the interim, Shīʿism was a rallying point for socially and politically discontented elements within the Muslim community. In addition to the Khārijites, another minority sect was thus formed, hostile from the beginning to the Umayyad government that seized power on ʿAlī's death. The majority of Muslims avoided both the Shīʿite and Khārijite positions, following instead the sunnah, or "practice," as these believers conceived the Prophet to have left it and as Abū Bakr, ʿUmar, ʿUthmān, and ʿAlī, too—known as *al-khulafāʾ al-rāshidūn* (Arabic: "the rightly guided caliphs")—had observed and codified it.

Abū Muslim's revolutionary movement was, as much as anything, representing Medinese mercantile interests in the Hejaz, dissatisfied with Umayyad inability to shelter Middle Eastern trade under a Pax Islamica. To promote the revolution aimed to destroy Umayyad power, the movement exploited Shīʿite aspirations and other forces of disenchantment. The Khārijites were excluded, since their movement opposed the idea of a caliphate of the kind Abū Muslim's adherents were fighting to establish—one that could command sufficient respect to hold together an Islamic universal state. A discontented element ready to fight for Abū Muslim's cause in Khorāsān, however, was not a religious grouping but Arab settlers and Iranian cultivators who were burdened by taxation.

In Iran the first Arab conquerors had concluded treaties with local Iranian magnates who had assumed authority when the Sāsānian imperial government disintegrated. These notables—the *marzbān*s and landlords (*dehqān*s)—undertook to continue tax collection on behalf of the new Muslim power. The advent of Arab colonizers, who preferred to cultivate the land rather than campaign farther into Asia, produced a further complication. Once the Arabs had settled in Iranian lands, they, like the Iranian cultivators, were required to pay the *kharāj*, or land tax, which was collected by Iranian notables for the Muslims in a system similar to that which had predated the conquest. The system was ripe for abuse, and the Iranian collectors extorted large sums, arousing the hostility of both Arabs and Persians.

Another source of discontent was the *jizyah*, or head tax, which was applied to non-Muslims of the tolerated religions—Judaism, Christianity, and Zoroastrianism. After they converted to Islam, Iranians expected to be exempt from this tax. But the Umayyad government, burdened with imperial expenses, often refused to exempt the Iranian converts.

The tax demands of the Damascus government were as distasteful to those urbanized Arabs and Iranians in commerce as they were to those in agriculture, and hopes of easier conditions under the new rulers than under the Sāsānids were not fully realized. The Umayyads ignored Iranian agricultural conditions, which required constant reinvestment to maintain irrigation works and to halt the encroachment of the desert. This no doubt made the tax burden, from which no returns were visible, all the more odious. Furthermore, the regime failed to maintain the peace so necessary to trade. Damascus feared the breaking away of remote provinces where the Arab colonists were becoming assimilated with the local populations. The government, therefore, deliberately encouraged tribal factionalism in order to prevent a united opposition against it.

Thus, the revolution set out to establish an Islamic ecumene above divisions and sectarianism, the Pax Islamica already referred to, which commerce required and which Iranian merchants without status in the Sāsānian social hierarchy looked to Islam to provide. Ease of communication from the Oxus (modern Amu Darya) River to the Mediterranean Sea was wanted but without what seemed like a nest of robbers calling themselves a government and straddling the route at Damascus. In 750 Umayyad power was destroyed, and the revolution gave the caliphate to the ʿAbbāsids.

Hejazi commercial interests had in a sense overcome the military party among leading Muslim Arabs. Greater concern for the east was manifested by the new caliphate's choice of Baghdad as its capital—situated on the Tigris a short distance north of Ctesiphon and designed as a new city, to be free of the factions of the old Umayyad garrison cities of Al-Kūfah, Wāsiṭ, and Al-Baṣrah.

The 'Abbāsid Caliphate (750–821)

The revolution that established the 'Abbāsids represented a triumph of the Islamic Hejazi elements within the empire; the Iranian revival was yet to come. Nevertheless, 'Abbāsid concern with fostering eastern Islam made the new caliphs willing to borrow the methods and procedures of statecraft employed by their Iranian predecessors. At Damascus the Umayyads had imitated Sāsānian court etiquette, but at Baghdad Persianizing influences went deeper and aroused some resentment among the Arabs, who were nostalgic for the legendary simplicity of human relations among the desert Arabs of yore. Self-conscious schools of manners grew up in the new metropolis, representing the competitive merits of the Arabs' or Persians' ancient ways.

To counter the widespread Arab chauvinism still present after the 'Abbāsid revolution, there arose a literary-political movement known as the *shu'ūbiyyah*, which celebrated the excellence of non-Arab Muslim peoples, particularly the Persians, and set the stage for the resurgence of Iranian literature and culture in the decades to come. Regard for poetry—the Arabs' vehicle of folk memory—increased, and minds and imaginations were quickened. Philosophical enquiry was developed out of the need for precision about the meaning of Holy Writ and for the establishment of the authenticity of the Prophet's dicta, collected as Hadith—sayings traditionally ascribed to him and recollected and preserved for posterity by his companions. An amalgam known as Islamic civilization was thus being forged in Baghdad in the 8th and 9th centuries.

The Iranian intellect, however, played a conspicuous part in what was still an Arab milieu. Works of Indian provenance were translated into Arabic from Pahlavi, the written language of Sāsānian Iran, notably by Ibn al-Muqaffaʿ (*c.* 720–756/57). The wisdom of both the ancient East and West was received and discussed in Baghdad's schools. The metropolis's outposts confronted Byzantium, as well as infidel marches in Afghanistan and Central Asia. Cultural influences came from both directions. Curiosity in the pursuit of knowledge had been enjoined by the Prophet "even as far as China." This cosmopolitanism was not new to the descendants of the urban Arabs of Mecca or to the Iranians, whose land lay across the routes from the Pacific to the Mediterranean. Both peoples knew how to transmute what was not originally their own into forms that were entirely Islamic. Islam had liberated men of the scribal and mercantile classes who in Iran had been subject to the dictates of a taboo-ridden and excessively ritualized Zoroastrianism and who in Arabia had been inhibited by tribal feuds and prejudices.

In spite of the development of a distinctive Islamic culture, the military problems of the empire were left unsolved. The ʿAbbāsids were under pressure from unbelievers on several fronts—Turks in Central Asia, pagans in India and in the Hindu Kush, and Christians in Byzantium. War for the faith, or jihad, against these infidels was a Muslim duty. But whereas the Umayyads had been expansionists and had seen themselves as heads of a military empire, the ʿAbbāsids were more pacific and saw themselves as the supporters of more than an Arab, conquering militia. Yet rebellions within the imperial frontiers had to be contained and the frontiers protected.

Rebellion within the empire took the form of peasant revolts in Azerbaijan and Khorāsān, coalesced by popular religious appeals centred on men who assumed or were accorded mysterious powers. Abū Muslim—executed in 755 by the second ʿAbbāsid caliph, al-Manṣūr, who feared his influence—became one such messianic figure. Another was al-Muqanna' (Arabic: "the Veiled One"), who used Abū Muslim's mystique and whose movement lasted from *c.* 775 to 780. The Khorram-dīnān (Persian: "Glad Religionists"), under the Azerbaijanian Bābak (816/17–38), also necessitated vigorous military suppression. Bābak eluded capture for two decades, defying the caliph in Azerbaijan and western Persia, before being caught and brought to Baghdad to be tortured and executed. These heresiarchs revived such creeds as that of the anti-Sāsānid religious leader Mazdak (d. 528 or 529), expressive of social and millenarian aspirations that were later canalized into Sufism on the one hand and into Shīʿism on the other.

Sīstān, Iran's southeastern border area, had a tradition of chivalry as the ancient homeland of Iranian military champions. Their tales passed to posterity collectively in the deeds of Rostam, son of Zāl, in Ferdowsī's *Shāh-nāmeh*, the Persian national epic. On the route to India, Sīstān was also a centre of trade. Its agrarian masses were counterbalanced by an urban population whose economy could be bolstered by plunder gained through military forays into still non-Muslim areas under the rule of the southern Hephthalites—the Zunbīls of the Hindu Kush's southwestern flanks—whose command of trade routes with India had to be contested when the existing partnership in this command broke down.

Early exploitation of the province's agriculture by Arab governors had, however, debilitated the rural life, and Khārijites, who found refuge in Sīstān from the Umayyads, organized or attracted bands of local peasants and vagabonds who had strayed south from Khorāsān. The presence of these groups indicates agricultural depression following the first century of rule by nonagricultural Arabs who had failed to grasp the needs of the Iranian

al-Muqanna‘

Hāshim ibn Ḥākim—better known as al-Muqanna‘—was a religious leader, originally a fuller (cloth processor) from Merv, in Khorāsān, who led a revolt in that province against the ‘Abbāsid caliph al-Mahdī. Preaching a doctrine combining elements of Islam and Zoroastrianism, al-Muqanna‘ carried on warfare for about three years in the field and for two years longer in his fortress of Sanām before he was eventually defeated and committed suicide in 783. He was the hero of the narrative poem *Lalla Rookh* (1817) by Thomas Moore.

cultivators. Khārijite bands isolated the cities and threatened their supplies. Sīstān needed an urban champion who could come to terms with the Khārijites and divert them to what could legitimately be termed jihad across the border, forming the gangsters into a well-disciplined loyal army. Such a man was Ya‘qūb ibn Layth, who founded the Ṣaffārid dynasty and threatened the Muslim empire with the first resurgence of Iranian independence.

THE "IRANIAN INTERMEZZO" (821–1055)

Ya‘qūb ibn Layth's movement differed from Ṭāhir ibn al-Ḥusayn's establishment of a dynasty of Iranian governors over Khorāsān in 821. The latter's rise marks the caliph's recognition, after the difficulties encountered in Iran by Hārūn al-Rashīd (ruled 786–809), that the best way for the imam and *amīr al-mu'minīn* at Baghdad to ensure military effectiveness in eastern Islam was by appointing a great general to govern Khorāsān. Ṭāhir had won Baghdad from Hārūn's son al-Amīn in favour of his other son, al-Ma'mūn, in the civil war between the two after their father's death. Ṭāhir was descended from the *mawālī* of an Arab leader in eastern Khorāsān. He was, therefore, of Iranian origin, but, unlike Ya'qūb, he did not emerge out of his own folk and because of a regional need. Instead, he rose as a servant of the caliphate, as whose lieutenant he was, in due course, appointed to govern a great frontier province. He made Neyshābūr his capital.

Though he died shortly after gaining the right of having his name mentioned after the caliph's in the *khuṭbah* (the formal sermon at the Friday congregations of Muslims when those with authority over the community were mentioned after the Prophet), his family was sufficiently influential and respected at Baghdad to retain the governorship of Neyshābūr until the Ṭāhirids were ousted from the city by Ya'qūb in 873. Thereafter they retired to Baghdad.

Discussion of the rise of "independent" Persian dynasties such as the Ṭāhirid in the 9th century has to be qualified: Not only does the skillful 'Abbāsid statecraft need to be considered, but also the Muslims' need for legality in a juridical-religious setting must be recognized. The majority of Muslims considered the caliph to be the legitimate head of the faith and the guarantor of the law. Such a guarantee was preeminently the need of merchants in the cities of Sīstān, Transoxania, and central Iran.

In the Caspian provinces of Gīlān and Ṭabaristān (Māzandarān), the situation was different. The Elburz Mountains had been a barrier against the integration of these areas into the Caliphate. Small princely families—the Bāvands, including the Kā'ūsiyyeh and the Espahbadiyyeh (665–1349), and the Musāfirids, also known as Sallārids or Kangarids (916–*c.* 1090)—had remained independent of the caliphal capitals, Damascus and Baghdad, in the mountains of Daylam. When Islam reached these old Iranian enclaves, it was brought by Shī'ite leaders in flight from metropolitan persecution. It was not the Islam of the Sunni state.

The Ṣaffārids

Ya'qūb ibn Layth began life as an apprentice *ṣaffār* (Arabic: "coppersmith"), hence his dynasty's name, Ṣaffārid. Taking to military freebooting, he mustered an army that he disciplined and regularly paid in cash, absorbing many Khārijites into its ranks. This and his extension of Islam into pagan areas of Sind and Afghanistan earned him the caliph's gratitude, which Ya'qūb courted by sending golden idols captured from infidels to be paraded in Baghdad.

Ya'qūb's attitude toward the imam's claiming political subservience was, nevertheless, strikingly similar to that of the caliph-rejecting Khārijites. He turned his attention inward instead of outside the pale of Islam. He seized Baghdad's breadbaskets—Fārs and Khūzestān—and drove the Ṭāhirid emir from Neyshābūr. His march on Baghdad itself was halted only by the stratagem devised by the caliph's commander in chief, who inundated Ya'qūb's army by bursting dikes. Ya'qūb died soon after, in 879. He had made an empire, minted his own coinage, fashioned a new style of army loyal to its leader rather than to any religious or doctrinal concept, and required that verses in his praise be put into his own language—Persian—from Arabic, which he did not understand. He began the Iranian resurgence.

The collapse of the Ṭāhirid viceroyalty left Baghdad faced with a power vacuum in Khorāsān and southern Persia. The caliph reluctantly confirmed Ya'qūb's brother 'Amr as governor of Fārs and Khorāsān but withdrew his recognition on three occasions, and 'Amr's authority was disclaimed to the Khorāsānian pilgrims to Mecca when they passed through Baghdad. But 'Amr remained useful to

Baghdad so long as Khorāsān was victimized by the rebels Aḥmad al-Khujistānī and, for longer, Rāfi' ibn Harthama. After Rāfi' had been finally defeated in 896, 'Amr's broader ambitions gave the caliph al-Mu'taḍid his chance. 'Amr conceived designs on Transoxania, but there the Sāmānids held the caliph's license to rule, after having nominally been Ṭāhirid deputies. When 'Amr demanded and obtained the former Ṭāhirid tutelage over the Sāmānids in 898, Baghdad could leave the Ṣaffārid and Sāmānid to fight each other, and the Sāmānid Ismā'īl (ruled 892–907) won. 'Amr was sent to Baghdad, where he was put to death in 902. His family survived as Sāmānid vassals in Sīstān and were heard of until the 16th century. Ya'qūb remains a popular hero in Iranian history.

The Sāmānids

There was nothing of the popular hero in the Sāmānids' origin. Their eponym was Sāmān-Khodā, a landlord in the district of Balkh and, according to the dynasty's claims, a descendant of Bahrām Chūbīn, the Sāsānian general. Sāmān became Muslim. His four grandsons were rewarded for services to the caliph al-Ma'mūn (ruled 813–833) and received the caliph's investiture for areas that included Samarkand and Herāt. They thus gained wealthy Transoxanian and east Khorāsānian entrepôt cities, where they could profit from trade that reached across Asia, even as far as Scandinavia, and from providing Turkish slaves—much in demand in Baghdad as royal troops—while they protected the frontiers and provided security for merchants in Bukhara, Samarkand, Khujand, and Herāt. With one transitory exception, they upheld Sunnism and at each new accession to power paid a tribute to Baghdad for the tokens of investiture from the caliph whereby their rule represented lawful authority. Thus, legal transactions in Sāmānid realms would be valid, and Baghdad received tribute in return for the insignia prayed over and signed by the caliph.

This tribute took the place of regular revenue, so that it represented a solution of the taxation problems and consequent resentments that had bedeviled the Umayyad regime. In modern assessments of imperial power, Baghdad may seem to have been politically the weaker for this type of arrangement, but ensuring the reign of Islam in peripheral provinces was important to the caliphs. Islam's portals to East Asia were adequately guarded, the supply of Turkish slaves essential for the caliph's bodyguard was maintained, and Turkish pagan tribes were converted to Islam under the Sāmānids.

The Iranian Renaissance

The Sāmānid aura lasted from 819 until it was eclipsed in 999. Its supremacy in northeastern Islam began in 875, when the Sāmānid emir, Naṣr I, received the license to govern all of Transoxania. Sāmānid emirs succeeded the Ṭāhirid-Ṣaffārid power in Khorāsān, and under them the Iranian renaissance at last came to fruition. Shaped out of the vernacular of northeastern Iranian courts and households and making skillful use of additional Arabic vocabulary, the Persian language emerged as a literary medium. Persian notation had been used in the first Muslim *dīwān*s, or chancelleries, in accountancy, because the first civil servants in the old Iranian areas had been Iranians. In 697 the ruthless Umayyad governor Ḥajjāj ibn Yūsuf had ordered the change to Arabic notation, marking the final dethronement of Pahlavi characters. When Modern Persian began to develop as a written language two centuries later, its alphabet was Arabic. It emerged as poetry, by which it was disciplined into a most expressive and flexible tongue, with the flexibility resulting from perfect control of a highly formal medium. The discipline was that of Arabic prosody, to which scenes of a verdure unknown to the Arab poet in the desert added, in the words of Iranian poets, a new and lustrous imagery. Rivaling the Arabs' tales of ancient valour was the Iranian legend versified under Sāmānid patronage in the *Shāh-nāmeh* ("Book of Kings"), Iran's national epic, composed by Ferdowsī of Ṭūs in Khorāsān over a 30-year period and finally completed after the eclipse of the Sāmānids, in 1009/10.

Shāh-nāmeh

The *Shāh-nāmeh* (Persian: "Book of Kings") is a celebrated work of the epic poet Ferdowsī, in which the Persian national epic found its final and enduring form. Written for Sultan Maḥmūd of Ghazna and completed in 1009/10, the *Shāh-nāmeh* is a poem of nearly 60,000 verses, mainly based on the *Khvatay-nāmak*, a history of the kings of

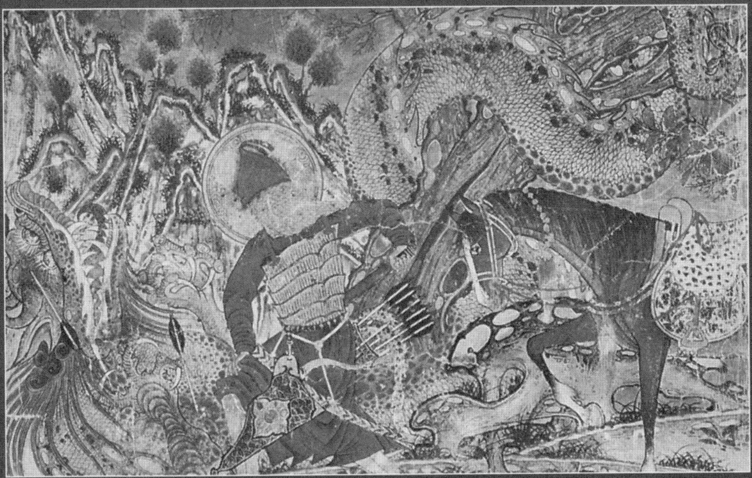

Bahrām V, also known as Bahrām Gūr, killing a dragon in an illustration from the Shāh-nāmeh, 1320–60; in the Cleveland Museum of Art. Courtesy of the Cleveland Museum of Art, Ohio, Grace Rainey Rogers Fund

Persia in Pahlavi (Middle Persian) from mythical times down to the 7th century. Ferdowsī versified and updated the story to the downfall of the Sāsānian empire (mid-7th century), and, for more than 1,000 years, it has remained one of the most popular works in the Persian-speaking world.

Under the Sāmānids, Bukhara rivaled Baghdad as a cultural capital of Islam. Besides the Persian poet Rūdakī (died 940/41), who had crystallized the language and imagery of Persian lyrical poetry as Ferdowsī (died between 1020 and 1026) was to do for that of the epic, patrons such as Naṣr II (ruled 914–943) attracted poets and scholars to Bukhara, many producing literary and academic works in both Persian and Arabic. A written Persian evolved that has survived with remarkably little change.

The Ghaznavids

Rūdakī, in a poem about the Sāmānid emir's court, describes how "row upon row" of Turkish slave guards were part of its adornment. From these guards' ranks two military families arose—the Sīmjūrids and Ghaznavids—who ultimately proved disastrous to the Sāmānids. The Sīmjūrids received an appanage in the Kūhestān region of southern Khorāsān. Alp Tigin founded the Ghaznavid fortunes when he established himself at Ghazna (modern Ghaznī, Afghanistan) in 962. He and Abū al-Ḥasan Sīmjūrī, as Sāmānid generals, competed with each other for the governorship of Khorāsān and control of the Sāmānid empire by placing on the throne emirs they could dominate. Abū al-Ḥasan died in 961, but a court party instigated by men of the scribal class—civilian ministers as contrasted with Turkish generals—rejected Alp Tigin's candidate for the Sāmānid throne. Manṣūr I was installed, and Alp Tigin prudently retired to his fief of Ghazna. The Sīmjūrids enjoyed control of Khorāsān south of the Oxus but were hard-pressed by a third great Iranian dynasty, the Būyids, and were unable to survive the collapse of the Sāmānids and the rise of the Ghaznavids.

The struggles of the Turkish slave generals for mastery of the throne with the help of shifting allegiance from the court's ministerial leaders both demonstrated and accelerated the Sāmānid decline. Sāmānid weakness attracted into Transoxania the Qarluq Turks, who had recently converted to Islam. They occupied Bukhara in 992 to establish in Transoxania the Qarakhanid, or Ilek Khanid, dynasty. Alp Tigin had been succeeded at Ghazna by Sebüktigin (d. 997). Sebüktigin's son Maḥmūd made an agreement with the Qarakhanids whereby the Oxus was recognized as their mutual boundary. Thus, the Sāmānids' dominion was divided and Maḥmūd was freed to advance westward into Khorāsān to meet the Būyids.

The Būyids

The Būyids (or Buwayhids) share with the Sāmānids the palm for having brought to fruition the Iranian renaissance. They achieved Iranian political reascendancy by doing what Ya'qūb ibn Layth had failed to do and what the Sāmānids would probably have considered illegal to do, namely, capturing Baghdad and making the caliph their puppet. As far east as the city of Rayy, western, central, and southern Iran were once more ruled by an Iranian dynasty. At the peak of the Būyid empire, the Būyid base second to Baghdad became Fārs, whence the Achaemenids and the Sāsānids had sprung. Politically, the Būyids effected the Iranianization of the metropolitan government in Baghdad. Yet, by the very fact that they saw in the caliphate an institution of enough purely political significance to merit its dramatic takeover, they paradoxically left the caliphate's political role emphasized by what at first sight might seem to have been deepest humiliation. Spiritually, the caliphate held no appeal for the Būyids, who were Shīʿite. Politically and juridically, as the stabilizing factor over the Islamic peoples, the Būyids, in spite of their own religious affiliation, maintained the caliphate.

The homeland of the Būyids was Daylam, in the Gīlān uplands in northern Iran. There, at the end of the 9th century, hardy valley dwellers had been stirred into martial activity by a number of factors, among them the rebel Rāfiʿ ibn Harthama's attempt to penetrate the region, ostensibly with Sāmānid support. 'Amr ibn Layth had pursued the rebel into the region. Other factors had been the formation of Shīʿite principalities in the area and continued Sāmānid attempts to subjugate them. After the Ṭāhirid collapse, the lack of stability in northern Iran south of the Elburz Mountains attracted many Daylamite mercenaries into the area on military adventures. Among them Mākān ibn Kākī served the Sāmānids with his compatriots, the sons of Būyeh, and their allies the Ziyārids under Mardāvīj. Mardāvīj introduced the three Būyid brothers to the Iranian plateau, where he established an empire reaching as far south as Eṣfahān and Hamadān. He was murdered in 935, but his Ziyārid descendants sought Sāmānid protection. They adhered to Sunnism and maintained themselves in the region southeast of the Caspian Sea. The Ziyārid Qābūs ibn Voshamgīr (ruled 978–1012) built himself a tomb tower, the Gonbad-e Qābūs (1006–07), which remains one of Iran's finest monuments. Also still extant is a work of his descendant ʿUnṣur al-Maʿālī Keykāʾūs (ruled 1049–90), the *Qābūs-nāmeh*, a prose "Mirror for Princes," which is a valuable document on the social and political life of the time.

Mardāvīj's expansionism south of the Elburz was taken up by his Būyid lieutenants: the eldest brother, 'Alī, consolidated power for himself in Eṣfahān and Fārs and obtained the caliph's recognition; another brother, Ḥasan, occupied Rayy and Hamadān; and the youngest brother, Aḥmad, took Kermān in the southeast and Khūzestān in the southwest. The caliphs al-Muttaqī and al-Mustakfī of the 940s were at the mercy of the Turkish slaves in their palace guard. The generals of the guard competed with each other for the office of *amīr al-umarā'* (commander in chief), who virtually ruled Iraq on behalf of the caliphs. When Aḥmad gained Khūzestān, he was close to the scene of the *amīr al-umarā'* contests, which he chose to settle by himself. Aḥmad entered Baghdad in 945 and assumed control of the caliphate's political functions. The caliph became a Būyid protégé and conferred on Aḥmad the title of Mu'izz al-Dawlah. 'Alī became 'Imād al-Dawlah, and Ḥasan became Rukn al-Dawlah. All these titles implied that the Būyids were the upholders of the Muslim 'Abbāsid *dawlah*, or state. In practice, however, the *dawlah* became a Daylamite state. It should be noted that the titles the caliph assigned the Būyids did not include the word *dīn*, or religion (as in Ṣalāḥ al-Dīn, "Righteousness of Religion"), which the caliph awarded exclusively to Sunni officials, thus emphasizing the continuing independence of the caliphate as a religious institution.

Later Būyid titles increased in grandeur. Even the old Achaemenian title of *shāhanshāh*, king of kings, reappeared—a title Aḥmad may have thought appropriate for an Iranian whose family reconquered Iran south of the Elburz Mountains. As suggested above, Būyid titles emphasized political and territorial sovereignty. This sovereignty reached its greatest extent under Rukn al-Dawlah's son, 'Aḍud al-Dawlah, who, after the deaths of his father and uncles, ruled an empire that comprised all of Persia west and south of Khorāsān and included Iraq, with Baghdad at its heart. ʿAḍud al-Dawlah pursued peace negotiations with Byzantium, perhaps to free himself for his cherished project of an Egyptian campaign against the rival caliphate of the Shīʿite Fāṭimids, established in North Africa in 909, which had been relocated in Egypt in 969. ʿAḍud al-Dawlah's concern with the middle kingdom and its westward extension toward the Mediterranean increased his hostility toward the Fāṭimids, in spite of his own Shīʿite persuasion. In the north he drove the Ziyārids out of Ṭabaristān, which struck a blow against the Sāmānids' influence in the Caspian area.

ʿAḍud al-Dawlah is celebrated for public works, of which the dam he built across the Kor River near Shīrāz, the Band-e Amīr ("Prince's Dam"), remains. He embellished the tomb of ʿAlī at Al-Najaf in Iraq, where he himself was also buried. He built libraries, schools, and hospitals, and he was the patron of the Arabic poet al-Mutanabbī. Some Arabic verses of his own are still extant. Although ʿAḍud al-Dawlah was undoubtedly one of Iran's greatest rulers, his fratricidal wars, conducted with terrible intractability on his way to power, initiated Būyid decline. The descendants of the early Būyids reversed the mutual fidelity of the first three brothers. The power this fidelity had achieved and ʿAḍud al-Dawlah had made into a world force crumbled after his death in 983.

His base had been Shīrāz, which he beautified and established as a cultural centre, but he died at Baghdad, where he chose to keep close to the caliph, whose daughter he married and from whom he took the title "the Crown of the Community" and the privilege, like the caliph, of having drums beaten at his gate on the calls to prayer. He also had his name mentioned after that of the caliph al-Ṭāʾiʿ in the *khuṭbah*. The Būyids avoided the policy, which in all likelihood would have disrupted the empire, of favouring the Shīʿites. Instead, they offered consolations of an emotional sort to the Shīʿites in the form of public rites on the anniversaries of the Shīʿite martyrs, notably the one commemorating the massacre of ʿAlī's son al-Ḥusayn and his followers under the Umayyads at Karbalāʾ in Iraq.

Although the Būyids were careful to avoid sectarian strife, family quarrels weakened them sufficiently for Maḥmūd of Ghazna to gain Rayy in 1029. But Maḥmūd (ruled 998–1030) went no farther: His dynasty paid great deference to the caliphate's legitimating power, and he made no bid to contest the Būyids' role as its protectors. Maḥmūd's agreement with the Sāmānids' Qarakhanid successors, that the Oxus should be their mutual boundary, held, but south of the river the Ghaznavids had to contend with their own distant relatives, the Oghuz Turks. Contrary to the sage counsel of Iranian ministers, Maḥmūd and his successor Masʿūd (ruled 1031–41) permitted these tribesmen to use Khorāsānian grazing grounds, which they entered from north of the Oxus. United under descendants of an Oghuz leader named Seljuq, between 1038 and 1040 these nomads drove the Ghaznavids out of northeastern Iran. The final encounter was at Dandānqān in 1040.

After their defeat by the Seljuqs, the Ghaznavids, patrons of Islamic culture and letters, were deflected eastward into India, where Maḥmūd had already conducted successful raids. The raids took the form of jihad (or holy war), and the Ghaznavids carried Islam and Persian Muslim art to the Indian subcontinent.

FROM THE SELJUQS TO THE MONGOLS

Ṭoghrıl Beg, the Seljuq sultan, entered Baghdad in 1055, and Būyid power was terminated, thus ending what Vladimir

Minorsky, the great Iranologist, called the "Iranian intermezzo." In Iran it was now the Seljuqs' turn to create a new imperial synthesis with the 'Abbāsid caliphs.

The Seljuqs

Ṭoghrıl I had proclaimed himself sultan at Neyshābūr in 1038 and had espoused strict Sunnism, by which he gained the caliph's confidence and undermined the Būyid position in Baghdad. The Oghuz Turks had accepted Islam late in the 10th century, and their leaders displayed a convert's zeal in their efforts to restore a Muslim polity along Sunni lines. Their efforts were made all the more urgent by the spread of Fāṭimid Ismā'īlī propaganda (Arabic: *da'wah*) in the eastern Caliphate by means of an underground network of propagandists, or *dā'īs*, intent on undermining the Būyid regime, and by the threat posed by the Christian Crusaders.

The Būyids' usurpation of the caliph's secular power had given rise to a new theory of state formulated by al-Māwardī (d. 1058). Al-Māwardī's treatise partly prepared the theoretical ground for Ṭoghrıl's attempt to establish an orthodox Muslim state in which conflict between the caliph-imam's spiritual-juridical authority on the one side and the secular power of the sultan on the other could be resolved, or at least regulated, by convention. Al-Māwardī reminded the Muslim world of the necessity of the imamate; but the treatise realistically admitted the existence of, and thus accommodated, the fact of military usurpation of power. The Seljuqs' own political theorist al-Ghazālī (died 1111) carried this admission further by explaining that the position of a powerless caliph, overshadowed by a strong Seljuq master, was one in which the latter's presence guaranteed the former's capacity to defend and extend Islam.

The caliph al-Qā'im (ruled 1031–75) replaced the last Būyid's name, al-Malik al-Raḥīm, in the *khuṭbah* and on the coins with that of Ṭoghrıl Beg; and after protracted negotiation ensuring restoration of the caliph's dignity after Shī'ite subjugation, Ṭoghrıl entered Baghdad in December 1055. The caliph enthroned him and married a Seljuq princess. After Ṭoghrıl had campaigned successfully as far as Syria, he was given the title of "king of the east and west." The new situation was justified by the theory that existing practice was legal whereby a new caliph could be instituted by the sultan, who possessed effective power and sovereignty, but that thereafter the sultan owed the caliph allegiance because only so long as the caliph-imam's juridical faculties were recognized could government be valid.

Ṭoghrıl Beg died in 1063. His heir, Alp-Arslan, was succeeded by Malik-Shah in 1072/73, and the latter's death in 1092 led to succession disputes out of which Berk-Yaruq emerged triumphant to reign until 1105. After a brief reign, Malik-Shah II was succeeded by Muḥammad I (ruled 1105–18). The last "Great Seljuq" was Sanjar (ruled 1118–57), who had earlier been governor of Khorāsān.

Alp-Arslan had nearly annihilated the Byzantine army at Manzikert in 1071, opening Asia Minor to those dependent tribesmen of the Seljuqs of whom Iran and the world were to hear more in the period of Ottoman power. Transoxania was subdued, the Christians in the Caucasus chastised, and the Fāṭimids expelled from Syria. An empire was for a short time achieved whose extent and stability enabled Alp-Arslan's and Malik-Shah's great minister, Niẓām al-Mulk (d. 1092), to pay a ferryman on the Oxus River with a draft cashable in Damascus.

Building and maintaining such a great empire necessitated a military regime and a vast war machine. The price to be paid later was oppression by military commanders and their units, set free to compete with each other and harry the land after the machine fell out of the grasp of powerful sultans. The soldiers had been remunerated by grants of land called *iqṭā*ʿs, which were originally usufructuary but developed over time into hereditary properties. The grants later became nuclei out of which petty principalities grew with the decline of the central power. The cultivators were left at the mercy of military overlords in possession of the soil.

The great minister Niẓām al-Mulk was typical of the Iranian bureaucracy, which, in an area prone to invasion, was often called on to attempt to cushion the impact of the brute military force of nomadic invaders and contain it within the bounds of administrative, economic, and cultural feasibility. For his Turkish masters he wrote the *Seyāsat-nāmeh* ("Book of Government"), in which he urged the regulation of royal court procedures in line with Sāmānid models and the restriction of the arrogance and cupidity of the military fief holders. His book is the measure of the Seljuqs' failure to provide enduring stability and equitable government. Had they done so, such a work would have been unnecessary.

The Ismāʿīliyyah

Of one disruptive force Niẓām al-Mulk's book is dramatically descriptive, in terms betraying near panic. The Seljuqs failed to nip in the bud the power of the Ismāʿīliyyah, originally spread throughout the eastern Islamic world by clandestine Fāṭimid *dāʿīs*—many of whose cells later split from the mainstream of events in Egypt to become an independent organization within the Seljuq empire. This organization exercised power by terrorism, and the name given its adherents by Europeans in the Middle Ages, Assassins (from *ḥashīshī*, denoting a consumer of hashish), has become a common noun in English. Ismāʿīlī doctrine consisted of an esoteric system combining extremist (Arabic: *ghulāt*) Shīʿite beliefs and a complex theology heavily permeated by the form and content of Hellenistic philosophy. The Ismāʿīliyyah recognized only 7 of the imams in descent from ʿAlī and Fāṭimah, whereas the Ithnā ʿAsharī Shīʿism—that followed by the Būyids and the dominant sect of modern Iran—recognized 12.

The movement in Iran crystallized under the leadership of Ḥasan-e Ṣabbāḥ, who had been trained in Fāṭimid Egypt. In 1090 Ḥasan gained the castle of Alamūt in the Elburz Mountains, and the order's principal cells were thereafter situated, so far as possible, in similar impregnable mountain strongholds. From these centres, *fidāʾīs*, or devotees ready to sacrifice their lives, issued forth and permeated society, spreading their mission as peddlers and itinerant tailors and gaining influence among the urban artisan and weaving classes. They were also often able to win the confidence of many highly placed women and children, whom they could please with novelties of dress or toys. Niẓām al-Mulk himself was assassinated by one of the *fidāʾīs*, but it is possible that this was done with the connivance of one of Malik-Shah's wives, whose son the vizier did not support for the succession.

The Ismāʿīliyyah were able to puncture Seljuq power but not destroy it. In the end the Seljuq empire collapsed where it had begun—in Khorāsān, where Sultan Sanjar ultimately failed to control Turkmen tribes related to him by blood. Sanjar could not rely on military commanders his family had raised to high posts and had rewarded with land and provincial powers. The tribesmen refused to be coerced into paying taxes. In 1153 they captured the old sultan and, although allowing him all the respect of his regal position, kept him captive for three years.

The Khwārezm-Shahs

Atsiz was the military leader who, after Sultan Sanjar's capture in 1153, succeeded in supplanting Seljuq power in northeastern Iran. His ancestor, Anūştegin, had been keeper of Malik-Shah's kitchen utensils and had been rewarded with the governorship of Khwārezm on the Oxus, where he founded the Khwārezm-Shah dynasty (*c.* 1077–1231). Regions elsewhere in Iran, on the passing of Seljuq supremacy, became independent under *atabegs*, who were originally proxy fathers and tutors sent with young Seljuq princes when these were deputed to govern provinces. At first the *atabegs* took power in the names of Seljuq puppets. When this fiction lapsed, *atabeg* dynasties such as the Eldegüzids of Azerbaijan (*c.* 1137–1225) and Salghurids of Fārs (*c.* 1148–1282) split Iran into independent rival principalities.

The Salghurid court in Shīrāz especially fostered the arts, as parvenu, competitive courts are wont to do. The poet Sa'dī (d. 1292) was a contemporary in Shīrāz of the Salghurid *atabeg* Abū Bakr ibn Sa'd ibn Zangī (ruled 1231–60), whom he mentions by name in his *Būstān* ("The Orchard"), a book of ethics in verse. Abū Bakr's father, Sa'd, for whom Sa'dī took his pen name, conferred great prosperity on Shīrāz.

Sa'd ibn Zangī came to terms with the Khwārezm-Shahs. Their power in Transoxania was secured by acceptance of tributary status to the non-Muslim Karakitai empire of Central Asia. They endeavoured to emulate the Seljuqs by following an expansionist policy in Iran south of the Oxus. Sa'd ibn Zangī, in his relations with the Khwārezm-Shah, set the pattern his successor Abū Bakr followed later. These *atabeg*s saved Fārs from outright invasion by northern military powers by paying heavy tribute. This tribute was the price of Shīrāz's remaining the peaceful haven of the arts in which Sa'dī and after him Ḥāfeẓ (d. 1389/90) flourished, to continue the Persian literary tradition begun under the Sāmānids and continued under both the Ghaznavids and the Seljuqs.

The collapse of the Karakitai empire northeast of the Oxus was partly accelerated by the unsuccessful bid of Khwārezm-Shah 'Alā' al-Dīn Muḥammad (ruled 1200–20) to win Muslim approval while releasing himself from the Khwārezm-Shahs' humiliating tributary status to an infidel power. But the coup de grâce to the Karakitai empire was delivered by its own vassal from the east, the Mongol leader Küchlüg Khan, who from 1211 onward was to be a direct opponent of the Khwārezm-Shahs in Central Asia. The Karakitai had been defeated, but the situation on the Khwārezm-Shah's eastern border had worsened.

Meanwhile, Sultan 'Alā' al-Dīn Muḥammad quarreled with the caliph; he set up an anticaliph of his own and further antagonized his Muslim subjects, who were unremittingly suspicious of a regime once subject to the Karakitai infidels and whose Kipchak mercenary militia and brutal commanders brought cruelty and desolation wherever they marched. 'Alā' al-Dīn Muḥammad was unable to control his army leaders, who had tribal connections with such influential people at court as his own mother. The post-Karakitai wars between him and Küchlüg Khan damaged the safety of the Central Asian trade arteries from China to the West. The great Mongol leader Genghis Khan took Beijing in 1215 and, as lord of

China, was concerned with Chinese trade outlets. The situation between Küchlüg and the Khwārezm-Shah sultan afforded scope as well as a pretext for the Mongols' westward advance, if only to restore the flow of trade.

The Mongol Invasion

Misunderstanding of how essentially fragile Sultan 'Alā' al-Dīn Muḥammad Khwārezm-Shah's apparently imposing empire was, its distance away from the Mongols' eastern homelands, and the strangeness of new terrain all doubtless induced fear in the Mongols, and this might partly account for the terrible events with which Genghis Khan's name has ever since been associated. The terror his invasion brought must also be ascribed to his quest

An illustration from a 13th-century book by Rashīd al-Dīn, depicting the Iranian encampment of Genghis Khan. The Mongol leader turned to warfare there after two peaceful missions were massacred. The Bridgeman Art Library/Getty Images

for vengeance. Genghis Khan's first two missions to Khwārezm had been massacred; but the place of commercial motives in the Mongol's decision to march to the west is indicated by the fact that the first was a trade mission. The massacre and robbery of this mission at Utrār by one of 'Alā' al-Dīn Muḥammad's governors before it reached the capital made Genghis single out Utrār for especially savage treatment when the murder of his second, purely diplomatic, mission left him no alternative but war.

His guides were Muslim merchants from Transoxania. They had to witness one of the worst catastrophes of history. During 1220–21 Bukhara, Samarkand, Herāt, Ṭūs, and Neyshābūr were razed, and the whole populations were slaughtered. The Khwārezm-Shah fled, to die on an island off the Caspian coast. His son Jalāl al-Dīn survived until murdered in Kurdistan in 1231. He had eluded Genghis Khan on the Indus River, across which his horse swam, enabling him to escape to India. He returned to attempt restoring the Khwārezmian empire over Iran. However, he failed to unite the Iranian regions, even though Genghis Khan had withdrawn to Mongolia, where he died in August 1227. Iran was left divided, with Mongol agents remaining in some districts and local adventurers profiting from the lack of order in others.

The Il-Khans

A second Mongol invasion began when Genghis Khan's grandson Hülegü Khan crossed the Oxus in 1256 and destroyed the Assassin fortress at Alamūt. With the disintegration of the Seljuq empire, the Caliphate had reasserted control in the area around Baghdad and in southwestern Iran. In 1258 Hülegü besieged Baghdad, where divided counsels prevented the city's salvation. Al-Musta'ṣim, the last 'Abbāsid caliph of Baghdad, was trampled to death by mounted troops (in the style of Mongol royal executions), and eastern Islam fell to pagan rulers.

Hülegü hoped to consolidate Mongol rule over western Asia and to extend the Mongol empire as far as the Mediterranean, an empire that would span the Earth from China to the Levant. Hülegü made Iran his base, but the Mamlūks of Egypt (1250–1517) prevented him and his successors from achieving their great imperial goal, by decisively defeating a Mongol army at 'Ayn Jālūt in 1260. Instead, a Mongol dynasty, the Il-Khans, or "deputy khans" to the great khan in China, was established in Iran to attempt repair of the damage of the first Mongol invasion. The injuries Iran had suffered went deep, but it would be unfair to attribute them all to Ghengis Khan's invasion, itself the climax to a long period of social and political disarray under the Khwārezm-Shahs and dating from the decline of the Seljuqs.

The Il-Khanid dynasty made Azerbaijan its centre and established Tabrīz as its first capital until Solṭāniyyeh was built early in the 14th century. At first, repair and readjustment of a stricken society were complicated by the collapse of law. The caliphate, as the symbol of Muslim legality, had been eroded by 'Alā' al-Dīn Muḥammad and by its own withdrawal into a temporal state in Iraq and the Tigris-Euphrates estuary region. But it had retained enough vitality for Sultan Muḥammad's action in setting up an anticaliph to have alienated influential members of his subject people. After 1258 it was gone altogether, while Hülegü Khan showed considerable religious eclecticism and had, in any event, the *yāsā*, or tribal law, of Genghis Khan to apply as the law of the Mongol state, in opposition to, or side by side with, the Sharī'ah, the law of Islam.

The Il-Khans' religious toleration released Christians and Jews from their restrictions under the Islamic regime. Fresh talent thus became available, but competition for new favours marred what good effects this release might have had on interfaith relations. It took time for Iranian administrators to resume their normal role after the invasion and to restore some semblance of administrative order and stability. Their process was impeded by the paganism of the new conquerors as well as by jostling for influence among classes of the conquered, not in this instance exclusively Muslim. At the same time, a shattered agrarian economy was burdened by heavy taxes, those sanctioned by the Sharīʿah being added to by those the *yāsā* provided for, so that the pressure of exploitation was increased by Mongol tax innovations as well as by the invaders' cupidity.

The pressure was increased beyond the economy's endurance: the Il-Khanid government ran into fiscal difficulties. An experiment with paper currency, modeled on the Chinese money, failed under Gaykhatu (ruled 1291–95). Gaykhatu was followed briefly by Baydu (d. 1295), who was supplanted by the greatest of the Il-Khans, Maḥmūd Ghāzān (ruled 1295–1304). Ghāzān abandoned Buddhism—the faith in which his grandfather Abagha, Hülegü's successor (ruled 1265–82), had reared him—and adopted Islam. One of his chief ministers was also his biographer, Rashīd al-Dīn, of Jewish descent. He seems deliberately to have striven to present Ghāzān, whom he styles the "emperor of Islam" (*pādshāh-e eslām*), as a ruler who combined the qualities and functions of both the former caliphs and ancient Iranian "great kings."

Ghāzān made strenuous efforts to regulate taxes, encourage industry, bring wasteland into cultivation, and curb the abuses and arrogance of the military and official classes. Facilities for domestic and foreign merchants were furnished. Buildings were constructed and irrigation channels dug. Medicinal and fruit-bearing plants were imported and the cultivation of indigenous ones encouraged. Observatories were built and improved—a sure indication of concern with agricultural improvement, for seasonal planning required accurate calendars. He fostered Muslim sentiment by showing consideration for the sayyids, who claimed descent from the Prophet's family, and it seems probable that he wished to eradicate or overlay Shīʿite-Sunni sectarian divisiveness, for Ghāzān's Islam appears to have been designed to appeal equally to both persuasions. Any slight bias in favour of the Shīʿites might be attributed to a desire to capture the emotions and imagination of many of the humble people who had reacted against the Seljuqs' zeal for Sunnism and craved a teaching that included millennial overtones. Shīʿism had been liberated by the fall of the ʿAbbāsid Caliphate, and its belief in the reappearance of the 12th imam, who was to inaugurate peace and justice in the world, satisfied this popular craving for religious solace.

Ghāzān's work was carried on, but less successfully, by his successor Öljeitü (ruled 1304–16). Between 1317 and 1335, though he finally relinquished the expensive campaigns against Egypt for the opening to the Mediterranean, Abū Saʿīd was unable to keep the Il-Khanid regime consolidated, and it fell apart on his death. Ghāzān's brilliant reign survives only in the pages of his historian, Rashīd al-Dīn. Wars against Egypt and their own Mongol kinsmen in Asia had in fact hampered the Il-Khans in accomplishing a satisfactory reintegration of an Iranian polity.

Hülegü

(b. c. 1217—d. Feb. 8, 1265, Shāhī Island, Iran)

Hülegü—also spelled Hulagu—was a Mongol ruler in Iran who founded the Il-Khanid dynasty and, as part of a Mongol program of subduing the Islamic world, seized and sacked Baghdad, the religious and cultural capital of Islam. Some historians consider that he did more than anyone else to destroy medieval Iranian culture.

Hülegü, a grandson of Genghis Khan, was appointed by his brother Mangu Khan, the fourth great khan of the Mongols, to extend Mongol power in Islamic areas. Hülegü destroyed the fortress of the Assassins in 1256 at Alamūt in north central Iran. He then defeated the caliph's army and captured and executed al-Mustaʿṣim, the last of the ʿAbbāsid caliphs, and in 1258 he seized and largely destroyed Baghdad. He captured Syria but was decisively defeated by the Mamlūks at the battle of ʿAyn Jālūt in 1260. He then returned to Iran, settling in the province of Azerbaijan.

As the *atabegs* had done after the Seljuqs, Il-Khanid military emirs began to establish themselves as independent regional potentates after 1335. At first, two of them, formerly military chiefs in the Il-Khans' service, competed for power in western Iran, ostensibly acting on behalf of rival Il-Khanid puppet princes. Ḥasan Küchük (the Small) of the Chūpānids was eventually defeated by Ḥasan Buzurg (the Tall) of the Jalāyirids, who set up the Jalāyirid dynasty over Iraq, Kurdistan, and Azerbaijan; it lasted from 1336 to 1432. In Fārs, Il-Khanid agents, the Injuids, after a spell of power during which Abū Isḥāq Injū had been the poet Hāfeẓ's patron, were ousted by Abū Saʿīd's governor of Yazd, Mubāriz al-Dīn Muẓaffar. Thus, in 1353 Shīrāz became the Muẓaffarid dynasty's capital, which it remained until conquest by Timur in 1393.

THE TIMURIDS AND TURKMEN

Timur (Tamerlane) claimed descent from Genghis Khan's family. The disturbed conditions in Mongol Transoxania gave this son of a minor government agent in the town of Kesh the chance to build up a kingdom in Central Asia in the name of the Chagatai Khans, whom he eventually supplanted. Timur entered Iran in 1380 and in 1393 reduced the Jalāyirids after taking their capital, Baghdad. In 1402 he captured the Ottoman sultan, Bayezid I, near Ankara. He conquered Syria and then turned his attention to campaigns far to the east of his tumultuously acquired and ill-cemented empire. He died in 1405 on an expedition to China.

Timur left an awesome name and an ambiguous record of flights of curiosity into the realms of unorthodox religious beliefs, history, and every kind of inquiry concerning lands and peoples. He showed interest in Sufism, a form of Islamic mysticism that varied from a scholastic study of ascetic techniques for mastering the carnal self to complete abandonment of all forms of authority in the belief that faith alone is necessary for salvation. Sufism had increased in the disturbed post-Seljuq era as both the consolation and the refuge of desperate people. In Sufism Timur may have hoped to find popular leaders whom he could use for his own purposes. His encounters with such keepers of the consciences of harried, exploited, and ill-treated Iranians proved that they knew him perhaps better than he knew himself. Whatever his motives may have been, the reverse of stability was his legacy to Iran. His division of his ill-assimilated conquests among his sons served to ensure that an integrated Timurid empire would never be achieved.

The nearest a Timurid state came to being an integrated Iranian empire was under Timur's son Shah Rokh (ruled 1405–47), who endeavoured to weld Azerbaijan and western Persia to Khorāsān and eastern Persia to form a united Timurid state for a short and troubled period. He succeeded only in loosely controlling western and southern Iran from his beautiful capital at Herāt. Azerbaijan demanded three major military expeditions from this pacific sovereign and even so could not long be held. He made Herāt the seat of a splendid culture, the atelier of great miniature painters (Behzād notable among them), and the home of a revival of Persian poetry, letters, and philosophy. This revival was not unconnected with an effort to claim for an Iranian centre once more the palm of leadership in the propagation of Sunni ideology: Herāt sent copies of Sunni canonical works on request to Egypt. The reaction, in Shīʿism's ultimate victory under the Ṣafavid shahs of Persia, was, however, already being prepared.

Western Iran was dominated by the Kara Koyunlu, the "Black Sheep" Turkmen. In Azerbaijan they had supplanted their former masters, the Jalāyirids. Timur had put these Kara Koyunlu to flight, but in 1406 they regained their capital, Tabrīz. On Shah Rokh's death, Jahān Shah (ruled *c.* 1438–67) extended Kara Koyunlu rule out of the northwest deeper into Iran at the Timurids' expense. The Timurids relied on their old allies, the Kara Koyunlu's rival Turkmen of the Ak Koyunlu, or "White Sheep," clans, who had long been established at Diyarbakır in Turkey. The White Sheep acted as a curb on the Black Sheep, whose Jahān Shah was defeated by the Ak Koyunlu Uzun Ḥasan by the end of 1467.

Uzun Ḥasan (ruled 1457–78) achieved a short-lived Iranian empire and even briefly deprived the Timurids of Herāt. He was, however, confronted by a new power in Asia Minor—the Ottoman Turks. His relationship with the Christian emperor at Trebizond (Trabzon) through his Byzantine wife, Despina, involved Uzun Ḥasan in attempts to shield Trebizond from the ineluctable Ottoman advance. The Ottomans crushingly defeated him in 1473. Under his son Yaʿqūb (ruled 1478–90), the Ak Koyunlu state was subjected to fiscal reforms associated with a government-sponsored effort to reapply rigorous purist principles of Sunni Islamic rules for revenue collection. Yaʿqūb attempted to purge the state of taxes introduced under the Mongols and not sanctioned by the Muslim canon. But the inquiries made by the Sunni religious authorities antagonized the vested interests, damaged the popularity of the Ak Koyunlu regime, and discredited Sunni fanaticism.

THE ṢAFAVIDS (1501–1736)

The attempt to revive strict Sunni religious values through revenue reform or to effect the latter under the guise of religion no doubt gave impetus to the spread of Ṣafavid Shīʿite propaganda. Another factor must have been related to the same general economic decline that made Sultan Yaʿqūb's fiscal reforms necessary in the first place. Sheikh Ḥaydar led a movement that had begun as a Sufi order under his ancestor Sheikh Ṣafī al-Dīn of Ardabīl (1253–1334). This order may be considered to have originally represented a puritanical, but not legalistically so, reaction against what they perceived to be the sullying of Islam, the staining of Muslim lands, by the Mongol infidels. What began as a spiritual, otherworldly reaction against irreligion and the betrayal of spiritual aspirations developed into a manifestation of the Shīʿite quest for dominion over a Muslim polity.

By the 15th century, the Ṣafavid movement could draw on both the mystical emotional force of Sufism and the Shīʿite appeal to the oppressed populace to gain a large number of dedicated adherents. Sheikh Ḥaydar inured his numerous followers to warfare by leading them on expeditions from Ardabīl against Christian enclaves in the nearby Caucasus. He was killed on one of these campaigns. His son Ismāʿīl was to avenge his death and lead his devoted army to a conquest of Iran whereby Iran gained a great dynasty, a Shīʿite regime, and in most essentials its shape as a modern nation-state.

Gone were the days of rule by converted and zealous Sunni Turks or by Mongols of ambiguous spiritual allegiance. Iran was transformed by the swelling tide of Shīʿism, which bore Ismāʿīl to the throne his family was to occupy without interruption until 1722, in one of the greatest epochs of Iranian history.

Shah Ismāʿīl

In 1501 Ismāʿīl I (ruled 1501–24) supplanted the Ak Koyunlu in Azerbaijan. Within a decade he gained supremacy over most of Iran as a ruler his followers regarded as divinely entitled to sovereignty. The Ṣafavids claimed descent—on grounds that modern research has shown to be dubious—from the Shīʿite imams. Muslims in Iran, therefore, could regard themselves as having found a legitimate imam-ruler, who, as a descendant of ʿAlī, required no caliph to legitimate his position. Rather, Ṣafavid political legitimacy was based on the religious order's mixture of Sufi ecstaticism and Shīʿite extremism (Arabic: *ghulū*), neither of which was the dusty scholasticism of the Sunni or Shīʿite legal schools.

The dynasty's military success was based both on Ismāʿīl's skill as a leader and on the conversion of a number of Turkmen tribes—who came to be known as the Kizilbash (Turkish: "Red Heads") for the 12-folded red caps these tribesmen wore, representing their belief in the 12 imams—to this emotionally powerful Sufi-Shīʿite syncretism. The Kizilbash became the backbone of the Ṣafavid military effort, and their virtual deification of Ismāʿīl contributed greatly to his swift military conquest of Iran. In later years, though, extremist (*ghulāt*) zeal and its chiliastic fervour began to undermine the orderly administration of the Ṣafavid state. Ismāʿīl's attempt to spread Shīʿite propaganda among the Turkmen tribes of eastern Anatolia prompted a conflict with the Sunni Ottoman Empire.

Following Iran's defeat by the Ottomans at the Battle of Chāldirān in 1514, Ṣafavid expansion slowed, and a process of consolidation began in which Ismāʿīl sought to quell the more extreme expressions of faith among his followers. Such actions were largely preempted, however, by Ismāʿīl's death in 1524 at the age of 36.

The new Iranian empire lacked the resources that had been available to the caliphs of Baghdad in former times through their dominion over Central Asia and the West: Asia Minor and Transoxania were gone, and the rise of maritime trade in the West was detrimental to a country whose wealth had depended greatly on its position on important east-west overland trade routes. The rise of the Ottomans impeded Iranian westward advances and contested with the Ṣafavids' control over both the Caucasus and Mesopotamia. Years of warfare with the Ottomans imposed a heavy drain on the Ṣafavids' resources. The Ottomans threatened Azerbaijan itself. Finally, in 1639 the Treaty of Qaṣr-e Shīrīn (also called the Treaty of Zuhāb) gave Yerevan in the southern Caucasus to Iran and Baghdad and all of Mesopotamia to the Ottomans.

SHAH ʿABBĀS I

The Ṣafavids were still faced with the problem of making their empire pay. The silk trade, over which the government held a monopoly, was a primary source of revenue. Ismāʿīl's successor, Ṭahmāsp I (ruled 1524–76), encouraged carpet weaving on the scale of a state industry. ʿAbbās I (ruled 1587–1629) established trade contacts directly with Europe, but Iran's remoteness from Europe, behind the imposing Ottoman screen, made maintaining and promoting these contacts difficult and sporadic.

ʿAbbās also transplanted a colony of industrious and commercially astute Armenians from Jolfā in Azerbaijan to a new Jolfā adjacent to Eṣfahān, the city he developed and adorned as his capital. The Ṣafavids had earlier moved their capital from the vulnerable Tabrīz to Qazvīn. After eliminating the Uzbek menace from east of the Caspian Sea in 1598–99, ʿAbbās could move his capital south to Eṣfahān, more centrally placed than Qazvīn for control over the whole country and for communication with the trade outlets of the Persian Gulf. ʿAbbās engaged English help to oust the Portuguese from the island of Hormuz in 1622. He also strove to lodge Ṣafavid power strongly in

The Masjed-e Emām (Imam Mosque) in Eṣfahān, Iran. Ray Manley/Shostal Associates

Khorāsān. There, at Mashhad, he developed the shrine of ʿAlī al-Riḍā, the eighth Shīʿite imam, as a pilgrimage centre to rival Shīʿite holy places in Mesopotamia, where visiting pilgrims took currency out of Ṣafavid and into Ottoman territory.

Under ʿAbbās, Iran prospered. The monarch continued the policy begun under his predecessors of eradicating the old Sufi bands and *ghulāt* extremists whose support had been crucial in building the state. The Kizilbash were replaced by a standing army of slave soldiers loyal only to the shah, who were trained and equipped on European lines with the advice of the English adventurer Robert Sherley. Sherley was versed in artillery tactics and, accompanied by a party of cannon founders, reached Qazvin with his brother Anthony in 1598.

The bureaucracy, too, was carefully reorganized, but the seeds of the sovereignty's weakness lay in the royal house itself, which lacked an established system of inheritance by primogeniture. A reigning shah's nearest and most acute objects of suspicion were his own sons. Among them, brother plotted against brother over who should succeed on their father's death. Intriguers, ambitious for influence in a subsequent reign, supported one prince against another. ʿAbbās did not adopt the Ottoman sultans' practice of eliminating royal males by murder (as a child he had been within a hair's breadth of being a victim of such a policy). Instead, he instituted the practice of immuring infant princes in palace gardens away from the promptings of intrigue and the world at large. As a result, his successors tended to be indecisive men, easily dominated by powerful dignitaries among the Shīʿite ulama—whom the shahs themselves had urged to move in large numbers from the shrine cities of Iraq in an attempt to bolster Ṣafavid legitimacy as an orthodox Shīʿite dynasty.

The Afghan Interlude

Ḥusayn I (ruled 1694–1722) was of a pious temperament and was especially influenced by the Shīʿite divines, whose conflicting advice, added to his own procrastination, sealed the sudden and unexpected fate of the Ṣafavid empire. One Maḥmūd, a former Ṣafavid vassal in Afghanistan, captured Eṣfahān and murdered Ḥusayn in his cell in the beautiful madrasah (religious school) built in his mother's name.

The Afghan interlude was disastrous for Iran. In 1723 the Ottomans, partly to secure more territory and partly to forestall Russian aspirations in the Caucasus, took advantage of the disintegration of the Ṣafavid realm and invaded from the west, ravaging western Persia. Nadr, an Afshārid Turkmen from northern Khorāsān, was eventually able to reunite Iran, a process he began on behalf of the Ṣafavid prince Ṭahmāsp II (ruled 1722–32), who had escaped the Afghans. After Nadr had cleared the country of Afghans, Ṭahmāsp made him governor of a large area of eastern Iran.

Religious Developments

As in the case of the early Sunni caliphate, Ṣafavid rule had been based originally on both political and religious legitimacy, with the shah being both king and divine representative. With the later erosion of Ṣafavid central political authority in the mid-17th century, the power of the Shīʿite clergy in civil affairs—as judges, administrators, and court functionaries—began to grow, in a way unprecedented in Shīʿite history. Likewise, the ulama began to take a more active role in agitating against Sufism and other forms of popular religion, which remained strong in Iran, and in enforcing a more scholarly type of Shīʿism among the masses. The development of the *taʿziyyah*—a passion play commemorating the martyrdom of al-Ḥusayn and his family—and the practice of visits to the shrines and tombs of local Shīʿite leaders began during this period, largely at the prompting of the Shīʿite clergy.

These activities coincided with an escalated debate between Shīʿite scholars in Iran and Iraq over the role played by the clergy in interpreting Islamic precepts. One faction felt that the only sound source of legal interpretation was the direct teachings of the 12 infallible imams, in the form of their written and oral testaments (Arabic: *akhbār*, hence the name of the sect: the Akhbāriyyah). Their opponents, known as the Uṣūliyyah, held that a number of fundamental sources (*uṣūl*) should be consulted ,but that the final source for legal conclusions rested in the reasoned judgment of a qualified scholar, a *mujtahid*. The eventual victory of the Uṣūliyyah in this debate during the turbulent years at the end of the Ṣafavid empire was to have resounding effects on both the shape of Shīʿism and the course of Iranian history. The study of legal theory (*fiqh*), the purview of the *mujtahids*, became the primary field of scholarship in the Shīʿite world, and the rise of the *mujtahids* as a distinctive body signaled the development of a politically conscious and influential religious class not previously seen in Islamic history.

This rising legalism also facilitated the implementation of a theory that was first voiced in the mid-16th century by the scholars ʿAlī al-Karakī and Zayn al-Dīn al-ʿĀmilī, which called for the clergy to act as a general representative (*nāʾib al-ʿamm*) of the Hidden Imam during his absence, performing such duties as administering the poor tax (*zakāt*) and income tax (*khums*, "one-fifth"), leading prayer, and running Sharīʿah courts. A strong Ṣafavid state and the presence of influential Akhbārī scholars at first managed to suppress the execution of these ideas, but the complete collapse of central authority in Iran during the 18th century accelerated the already considerable involvement of the clerisy in state and civil affairs, a trend that would continue until modern times.

NĀDIR SHAH (1736–47)

Nadr later dethroned Ṭahmāsp II in favour of the latter's son, the more pliant 'Abbās III. His successful military exploits, however, which included victories over rebels in the Caucasus, made it feasible for this stern warrior himself to be proclaimed monarch—as Nādir Shah—in 1736. He attempted to mollify Persian-Ottoman hostility by establishing in Iran a less aggressive form of Shīʿism, which would be less offensive to Ottoman sensibilities; but this experiment did not take root. Nādir Shah's need for money drove him to embark on his celebrated Indian campaign in 1738–39. His capture of Delhi and of the Mughal emperor's treasure gave Nādir booty in such quantities that he was able to exempt Iran from taxes for three years. His Indian expedition temporarily solved the problem of how to make his empire financially viable.

How large this problem loomed in Nādir Shah's mind is demonstrated by his increasingly morbid obsession with treasure and jewels. After suspecting his son of complicity in a plot against him in 1741, Nādir Shah's mind seems to have become unhinged; his brilliance and courage deteriorated into a meanness and capricious cruelty that could no longer be tolerated. In 1747 he was murdered by a group of his own Afshārid tribesmen, together with some Qājār chiefs—a sad end to one of Iran's greatest leaders.

Nādir had been the first modern Iranian leader to perceive the importance of having his own navy, and in 1734 he had appointed an "admiral of the gulf." Ships were purchased from their British captains, and by 1735 the new Iranian navy had attacked Al-Baṣrah. What really mattered, however, were the land forces. Nādir Shah's reign exemplified the fact that, to be successful, a shah of Iran had to prove himself capable of defending his realm's territorial integrity and of extending its sources of wealth and production by conquest. To these ends, Nādir Shah built up a large army composed of tribal units under their own chiefs, such as his Afshārid kinsmen and the Qājār and Bakhtyārī.

But on Nādir Shah's death his great military machine dispersed, its commanders bent on establishing their own states. Aḥmad Shah Durrānī founded a kingdom in Afghanistan based in Kandahār. Shah Rokh, Nādir Shah's blind grandson, succeeded in maintaining himself at the head of an Afshārid state in Khorāsān, its capital at Mashhad. The Qājār chief Muḥammad Ḥasan took Māzanderān south of the Caspian Sea. Āzād Khan, an Afghan, held Azerbaijan, whence Moḥammad Ḥasan Khan Qājār ultimately expelled him. The Qājār chief, therefore, disposed of this post-Nādir Shah Afghan remnant in northwestern Iran but was himself unable to make headway against a new power arising in central and southern Iran, that of the Zands.

THE ZAND DYNASTY (1751–94)

Muḥammad Karīm Khan Zand entered into an alliance with the Bakhtyārī chief ʿAlī Mardān Khan in an effort to seize Eṣfahān—then the political centre of Iran—from Shah Rokh's vassal, Abū al-Fatḥ Bakhtyārī. Once this goal was achieved, Karīm Khan and ʿAlī Mardān agreed that Shah Sulṭān Ḥusayn Ṣafavī's grandson, a boy named Abū Ṭurāb, should be proclaimed Shah Ismāʿīl III in order to cement popular support for their joint rule. The two also agreed that the popular Abū al-Fatḥ would retain his position as governor of Eṣfahān, ʿAlī Mardān Khan would act as regent over the young puppet, and Karīm Khan would take to the field in order to regain lost Ṣafavid territory. ʿAlī Mardān Khan, however, broke the compact and was killed by Karīm Khan, who gained supremacy over central and southern Iran and reigned as regent or deputy (*vakīl*) on behalf of the powerless Ṣafavid prince, never arrogating to himself the title of shah. Karīm Khan made Shīrāz his capital and did not contend with Shah Rokh (ruled 1748–95) for the hegemony of Khorāsān. He concentrated on Fārs and the centre but managed to contain the Qājār in Māzanderān, north of the Elburz Mountains. He kept Āghā Moḥammad Khan Qājār a hostage at his court in Shīrāz, after repulsing Muḥammad Ḥasan Qājār's bids for extended dominion.

Karīm Khan's geniality and common sense inaugurated a period of peace and popular contentment, and he strove for commercial prosperity in Shīrāz, a centre accessible to the Persian Gulf ports and trade with India. After Karīm Khan's death in 1779, Āghā Moḥammad Khan escaped to the Qājār tribal country in the north, gathered a large force, and embarked on a war of conquest.

THE QĀJĀR DYNASTY (1796–1925)

Between 1779 and 1789 the Zands fought among themselves over their legacy. In the end it fell to the gallant Loṭf ʿAlī, the Zands' last hope. Āghā Moḥammad Khan relentlessly hunted him down until he overcame and killed him at the southeastern city of Kermān in 1794. In 1796 Āghā Moḥammad Khan assumed the imperial diadem, and later in the same year he took Mashhad. Shah Rokh died of the tortures inflicted on him to make him reveal the complete tally of the Afshārids' treasure. Āghā Moḥammad was cruel and he was avaricious.

Karīm Khan's commercial efforts were nullified by his successors' quarrels. With cruel irony, attempts to revive the Persian Gulf trade were followed by a British mission from India in 1800, which ultimately opened the way for a drain of Persian bullion to India. This drain was

Āghā Moḥammad Khan

(b. 1742, Gorgān, Iran—d. 1797, near Shusha)

Āghā Moḥammad Khan was the founder and first ruler of the Qājār dynasty of Iran. Following the disintegration of the Ṣafavid empire in 1722, Qājār tribal chieftains became prominent in Iranian affairs.

At the age of six Āghā Moḥammad was castrated on the orders of 'Ādil Shāh to prevent him from becoming a political rival, but this disability did not hinder his career. In 1757 he became the de facto governor of the Azerbaijan province of northern Iran; the next year he succeeded his father as chief of the Qavānlū clan of the Qājārs. In 1762 he was captured by a rival chieftain and sent as a prisoner to Shīrāz, where he spent the next 16 years as a political hostage. In 1779 Āghā Moḥammad escaped and fled to Astarābād, the centre of Qavānlū authority. By 1785, when Tehrān was made the capital, he was the dominant political figure in northern Iran.

In 1796 Āghā Moḥammad led a successful expedition against the Christian Kingdom of Georgia, which was then reincorporated into Iran. Crowned the same year as *shāhanshāh* ("king of kings"), he conquered Khorāsān, the last centre of resistance to his authority; its blind ruler, Shah Rokh (the grandson of Nādir Shah), was tortured to death.

The civil war that led to the establishment of the Qājār dynasty, followed by Āghā Moḥammad's conquests, had serious consequences for the prosperity and economy of Iran. Many cities, such as Kermān, were completely sacked. In monetary matters Āghā Moḥammad was tightfisted. The extraordinary cruelty of his reign was in part a means to deter rebellion. During his reign his capital city of Tehrān grew from a village to a city of about 15,000 people. While leading a second expedition into Georgia, Āghā Moḥammad was assassinated by two of his servants. The major legacies of his reign were a unified Iran and a dynasty that ruled it until 1925.

made inevitable by the damage done to Iran's productive capacity during Āghā Moḥammad Khan's campaigns to conquer the country.

The Age of Imperialism

Fatḥ 'Alī Shah (ruled 1797–1834), in need of revenue after decades of devastating warfare, relied on British subsidies to cover his government's expenditures. Following a series of wars, he lost the Caucasus to Russia by the treaties of Golestān in 1813 and Turkmanchay (Torkmān Chāy) in 1828, the latter of which granted Russian commercial and consular agents access to Iran. This began a diplomatic rivalry between Russia and Britain—with Iran the ultimate victim—that resulted in the 1907 Anglo-Russian Convention giving each side exclusive spheres of influence in Iran, Afghanistan, and Tibet.

The growth of European influence in Iran and the establishment of new transportation systems between Europe and the Middle East were followed by an unprecedented increase in trade that ultimately changed the way of life in both urban and rural areas of Iran. As with other semicolonized countries of this era, Iran became a source of cheap raw materials and a market for industrial goods from Western countries. A sharp drop in the export of manufactured commodities was accompanied by a significant rise in the export of raw materials such as opium, rice, tobacco, and nuts. This rapid change made the country more vulnerable to global market fluctuations and, because of an increase in acreage devoted to nonfood export crops, periodic famine. Simultaneously, in an effort to increase revenue, Qājār leaders sold large tracts of state-owned lands to private owners—most of whom were large merchants—subsequently disrupting traditional forms of land tenure and production and adversely affecting the economy.

Ḥājjī Mīrzā Āghāsī, a minister of Moḥammad Shah (ruled 1834–48), tried to activate the government to revive sources of production and to cement ties with lesser European powers, such as Spain and Belgium, as an alternative to Anglo-Russian dominance, but little was achieved. Nāṣer al-Dīn Shah (ruled 1848–96) made Iran's last effort to regain Herāt, but British intervention in 1856–57 thwarted his efforts. Popular and religious antagonism to the Qājār regime increased as Nāṣer al-Dīn strove to raise funds by granting foreign companies and individuals exclusive concessions over Iranian import and export commodities and natural resources in exchange for lump cash payments. The money paid for concessions was ostensibly for developing Iran's resources but instead was squandered by the court and on the shah's lavish trips to Europe.

Popular Protest and the Constitutional Revolution

In 1890 Nāṣer al-Dīn Shah granted a nationwide concession over the sale and importation of tobacco products to a British citizen. However, popular protest compelled Nāṣer al-Dīn to cancel the concession, demonstrating factors of crucial significance for the years to come: first, that there existed in Iran a mercantile class of sufficient influence to make use of such broad, popular sentiment; and second, that such public outpourings of discontent could limit the scope of the shah's power. More important, the protest demonstrated the growing power of the Shīʿite clergy, members of which had played a crucial role in rallying Iranians against the monopoly and which was to have great influence over political changes to come.

The "Tobacco Riots"—as this episode came to be known—were a prelude to the Constitutional Revolution that was to occur in the reign of Moẓaffar al-Dīn Shah

A relief image of Nāṣer al-Dīn, the shah whose actions sparked Iran's "Tobacco Riots," a precursor to the Constitutional Revolution of the early 20th century. Roger Viollet/Getty Images

(ruled 1896–1907), during a time when the country suffered deep economic problems associated with its integration into a world economy. Iran had remained on the silver standard after most countries had left bimetallism for a gold standard in the late 1860s. Silver values in Iran slipped from the 1870s onward, and silver bullion drained out of the country, which lead to high rates of inflation and to bread riots. Further, in 1898 the government retained a foreign adviser to restructure the Customs Bureau. That action increased government revenue but alarmed Iranian merchants who feared further tax increases, including a substantial land tax. Merchants and landowners appealed for help to the ulama, with whom they had traditionally maintained close ties. Many of the clergy had themselves become increasingly hostile to the Qājār regime because the clerics had become indignant over government interference in spheres that traditionally were administered by the clergy (such as the courts and education) and over fears that the government might tax *vaqf* land (mortmain, administered by the clergy). In a trend begun in the Ṣafavid period, a number of influential *mujtahid*s began to concern themselves with matters of government, to the point of questioning the regime's legitimacy. Even the shahs' earlier suppression of the Bābī and Bahāʾī movements, viewed as heresy by the majority of the Shīʿite establishment, failed to ingratiate the regime with the ulama. Together these groups—ulama, merchants, and landowners—began to criticize the privileges and protections accorded to European merchants and called for political and legal reforms.

At the same time, Iran was increasingly interacting with the West. This contact sparked an interest in democratic institutions among the members of a nascent intellectual class, which itself was a product of new, Western-style schools promoted by the shah. Encouraged by the Russian Revolution of 1905 and influenced by immigrant workers and merchants from Russian-controlled areas of Transcaucasia, the new Iranian intellectuals were, paradoxically, to find common cause with Iran's merchants and Shīʿite clergy.

All aggrieved parties found an opportunity for social reform in 1905–06 when a series of demonstrations, held in protest over the government beating of several merchants, escalated into strikes that soon adjourned to a shrine near Tehrān, which the demonstrators claimed as a *bast* (Persian: "sanctuary"). While under this traditional

Iranian form of sanctuary, the government was unable to arrest or otherwise molest the demonstrators, and a series of such sanctuary protests over subsequent months, combined with wide-scale general strikes of craftsmen and merchants, forced the ailing shah to grant a constitution in 1906. The first National Consultative Assembly (the Majles) was opened in October of that year. The new constitution provided a framework for secular legislation, a new judicial code, and a free press. All these reduced the power of the royal court and religious authorities and placed more authority in the hands of the Majles, which, in turn, took a strong stand against European intervention.

Although the Majles was suppressed in 1908 under Moḥammad ʿAlī Shah (ruled 1907–09) by the officers of the Persian Cossack Brigade—the shah's bodyguard and the most effective military force in the country at the time—democracy was revived the following year under the second Majles, and Moḥammad ʿAlī fled to Russia. Constitutionalists also executed the country's highest-ranking cleric, Sheikh Fażlullāh Nūrī, who had been found guilty by a reformist tribunal of plotting to overthrow the new order—an indication that not all of Iran's religious elite were proponents of reform. In addition, as part of the secular reforms introduced by the Majles, a variety of secular schools were established during that time, including some for girls, causing significant tension between sections of the clergy that had previously advocated reform and their erstwhile intellectual allies.

The end of the Majles, however, did not come as a result of internal strife. In an attempt to come to grips with Iran's ongoing financial problems, the Majles in 1911 hired another foreign financial adviser, this time an American, William Morgan Shuster, who advocated bold moves to collect revenue throughout the country. This action angered both the Russians and British, who claimed limited sovereignty in the respective spheres of influence the two powers had carved out of Iran in 1907 (the Russians in northern Iran and the Caucasus and the British along the Persian Gulf). The Russians issued an ultimatum demanding Shuster's dismissal. When the Majles refused, Russian troops advanced toward Tehrān, and the regent of the young Aḥmad Shah (ruled 1909–25) hastily dismissed Shuster and dissolved the Majles in December 1911.

THE RISE OF REZA KHAN AND THE PAHLAVI DYNASTY (1925–79)

Until the beginning of World War I, Russia effectively ruled Iran, but with the outbreak of hostilities, Russian troops withdrew from the north of the country, and Iranians convened the third Majles. Jubilation was short-lived, however, as the country quickly turned into a battlefield between British, German, Russian, and Turkish forces. The landed elite hoped to find in Germany a foil for the British and Russians, but change eventually was to come from the north.

Following the Russian Bolshevik Revolution in 1917, the new Soviet government unilaterally canceled the tsarist concessions in Iran, an action that created tremendous goodwill toward the new Soviet Union and, after the Central Powers were defeated, left Britain the sole Great Power in Iran. In 1919 the Majles, after much internal wrangling, refused a British offer of military and financial aid that effectively would have made Iran into a protectorate of Britain. The British were initially loath to withdraw from Iran but caved to international pressure and removed their advisers by 1921. In that same year British diplomats lent their support to an Iranian officer of the Persian Cossack Brigade, Reza Khan, who in the previous year had been instrumental in putting down a rebellion led by Mīrzā

Kūchak Khan, who had sought to form an independent Soviet-style republic in Iran's northern province of Gīlān. In collaboration with a political writer, Sayyid Ziya al-Din Tabataba'i, Reza Khan staged a coup in 1921 and took control of all military forces in Iran. Between 1921 and 1925 Reza Khan—first as war minister and later as prime minister under Aḥmad Shah—built an army that was loyal solely to him. He also managed to forge political order in a country that for years had known nothing but turmoil. Initially Reza Khan wished to declare himself president in the style of Turkey's secular nationalist president, Mustafa Kemal Atatürk—a move fiercely opposed by the Shīʿite ulama—but instead he deposed the weak Aḥmad Shah in 1925 and had himself crowned Reza Shah Pahlavi, so founding the short-lived Pahlavi dynasty.

Sayyid Ziya al-Din Tabataba'i

(b. c. 1888—d. Aug. 29, 1969, Tehrān)

Sayyid Ziya al-Din Tabataba'i was an Iranian statesman who led the coup d'état of 1921 in which he was made prime minister. He had become prominent during World War I as the editor of a pro-British newspaper, *Ra'd* ("Thunder"). In 1919 he led a quasi-diplomatic mission to negotiate a commercial agreement with the anti-Communist Russian revolutionaries at Baku. On his return to Iran he joined a secret nationalist society, created a coalition of anticommunist politicians, and masterminded the coup d'état of Feb. 21/22, 1921, that made him prime minister of Iran. Soon after assuming that office, he quarreled with the coup's military leader, Col. Reza Khan (who in 1925 became shah of Iran), and in May was forced into exile.

Tabataba'i spent the next 20 years in Palestine; after the abdication of Reza Shah in September 1941, he returned to Iran. In 1942 he was elected to the Iranian Parliament, and in 1943 he founded the pro-British, anticommunist National Will party, which was active until 1951, at which time Tabataba'i faded from the political scene.

REZA SHAH

During the reign of Reza Shah Pahlavi, educational and judicial reforms were effected that laid the basis of a modern state and reduced the influence of the religious classes. A wide range of legal affairs that had previously been the purview of Shīʿite religious courts were now either administered by secular courts or overseen by state bureaucracies, and, as a result, the status of women improved. The custom of women wearing veils was banned, the minimum age for marriage was raised, and strict religious divorce laws (which invariably favoured the husband) were made more equitable. The number and availability of secular schools increased for both boys and girls, and the University of Tehrān was established in 1934, further eroding what had once been a clerical monopoly on education.

Nonetheless, Reza Shah was selective on what forms of modernization and secularization he would adopt. He banned trade unions and political parties and firmly muzzled the press. Oil concessions were first granted in 1901, during the Qājār period, and the first commercially exploitable petroleum deposits were found in 1908. Reza Shah renegotiated a number of these concessions, in spite of the ire these agreements raised among the Iranian people. The concessions were to remain a violent point of contention in Iran for decades to come.

Reza Shah's need to expand trade, his fear of Soviet control over Iran's overland routes to Europe, and his apprehension at renewed Soviet and continued British presence in Iran drove him to expand trade with Nazi Germany in the 1930s. His refusal to abandon what he considered to be obligations to numerous Germans in Iran served as a pretext for an Anglo-Soviet invasion of his country in 1941. Intent on ensuring the safe passage of U.S. war matériel to the Soviet Union through Iran, the Allies forced Reza Shah to abdicate, placing his young son Mohammad Reza Shah Pahlavi on the throne.

Wartime and Nationalization of Oil

Mohammad Reza Shah succeeded to the throne in a country occupied by foreign powers, crippled by wartime inflation, and politically fragmented. Paradoxically, however, the war and occupation had brought a greater degree of economic activity, freedom of the press, and political openness than had been possible under Reza Shah. Many political parties were formed in this period, including the pro-British National Will and the pro-Soviet Tūdeh ("Masses") parties. These, along with a fledgling trade union movement, challenged the power of the young shah, who did not wield the absolute authority of his father. At the same time, the abdication of Reza Shah had strengthened conservative clerical factions, which had chafed under that leader's program of secularization.

Following the war, a loose coalition of nationalists, clerics, and noncommunist left-wing parties, known as the National Front, coalesced under Mohammad Mosaddeq, a career politician and lawyer who wished to reduce the powers of the monarchy and the clergy in Iran. Most important, the National Front, angered by years of foreign exploitation, wanted to regain control of Iran's natural resources. In March 1951 Mosaddeq's oil-nationalization act was passed by the Majles, and shortly thereafter he was appointed prime minister. Britain, the main benefactor of Iranian oil concessions, imposed an economic embargo on Iran and pressed the International Court of Justice to consider the matter.

The court, however, decided not to intervene, thereby tacitly lending its support to Iran.

In spite of this apparent success, Mosaddeq was under both domestic and international pressure. British leaders Winston Churchill and Anthony Eden pushed for a joint U.S.-British coup to oust Mosaddeq, and the election of Pres. Dwight D. Eisenhower in the United States in November 1952 bolstered those inside the U.S. Central Intelligence Agency (CIA) who wished to support such an action.

Within Iran, Mosaddeq's social democratic policies, as well as the growth of the communist Tūdeh Party, weakened the always-tenuous support of his few allies among Iran's religious class, whose ability to generate public support was important to Mosaddeq's government. In August 1953, following a round of political skirmishing, Mosaddeq's quarrels with the shah came to a head, and the Iranian monarch fled the country. Almost immediately, in spite of still-strong public support, the Mosaddeq government buckled during a coup funded by the CIA. Within a week of his departure, Mohammad Reza Shah returned to Iran and appointed a new prime minister.

Iranian statesman Mohammed Mosaddeq. Before becoming prime minister, Mosaddeq spearheaded an effort to nationalize Iranian oil and curb foreign exploitation of the country's national resources. Keystone/Hulton Archive/Getty Images

Nationalization under Mosaddeq had failed, and after 1954 a Western multinational consortium led by British Petroleum accelerated Iranian oil development. The National Iranian Oil Company (NIOC) embarked on a thorough expansion of its oil-production capacities. NIOC also formed a petrochemical subsidiary and concluded agreements, mainly on the basis of equal shares, with several international companies for oil exploitation outside the area of the consortium's operations.

Petroleum revenues were to fuel Iran's economy for the next quarter of a century. There was no further talk of nationalization, as the shah firmly squelched subsequent political dissent within Iran. In 1957, with the aid of U.S. and Israeli intelligence services, the shah's government formed a special branch to monitor domestic dissidents. The shah's secret police—the Organization of National Security and Information, Sāzmān-e Amniyyat va Ettela'āt-e Keshvār, known by the acronym SAVAK—developed into an omnipresent force within Iranian society and became a symbol of the fear by which the Pahlavi regime was to dominate Iran.

Mohammad Mosaddeq

(b. 1880, Tehrān, Iran—d. March 5, 1967, Tehrān)

Mohammad Mosaddeq (whose name is also sometimes spelled Masaddiq or Mossadegh) was an Iranian political leader who nationalized the huge British oil holdings in Iran and, as premier in 1951–53, almost succeeded in deposing the shah.

The son of an Iranian public official, Mosaddeq grew up as a member of Iran's ruling elite. He received a Doctor of Law degree from the University of Lausanne in Switzerland and then returned to Iran in 1914 and was appointed governor-general of the important Fārs province. He remained in the government following the rise to power of Reza Khan in 1921 and served as minister of finance and then briefly as minister of foreign affairs. Mosaddeq was elected to the Majles (parliament) in 1923. When Reza Khan was elected shah (as Reza Shah Pahlavi) in 1925, however, Mosaddeq opposed the move and was compelled to retire to private life.

Mosaddeq reentered public service in 1944, following Reza Shah's forced abdication in 1941, and was elected again to the Majles. An outspoken advocate of nationalism, he soon played a leading part in successfully opposing the grant to the Soviet Union of an oil concession for northern Iran similar to an existing British concession in southern Iran. He built considerable political strength, based largely on his call to nationalize the concession and installations in Iran of the British-owned Anglo-Iranian Oil Company. In March 1951 the Majles passed his oil-nationalization act, and his power had grown so great that the shah, Mohammad Reza Shah Pahlavi, was virtually forced to appoint him premier.

The nationalization resulted in a deepening crisis in Iran, both politically and economically. Mosaddeq and his National Front Party continued to gain power but alienated many supporters, particularly among the ruling elite and in the Western nations. The British soon withdrew completely from the Iranian oil market, and economic problems increased when Mosaddeq could not readily find alternate oil markets.

A continuing struggle for control of the Iranian government developed between Mosaddeq and the shah. In August 1953, when the shah attempted to dismiss the premier, mobs of Mosaddeq followers took to the streets and forced the shah to leave the country. Within a few days, however, Mosaddeq's opponents, with U.S. support, overthrew his regime and restored the shah to power. Mosaddeq was sentenced to three years' imprisonment for treason and, after he had served his sentence, was kept under house arrest for the rest of his life. The Iranian oil-production facilities remained under the control of the Iranian government.

Mosaddeq's personal behaviour—which included wearing pajamas for numerous public appearances, speeches to the Majles from his bed (which was taken into the chambers), and frequent bouts of public weeping—helped focus world attention upon him during his premiership. Supporters claim the behaviour was a result of illness; detractors say he had a shrewd sense of public relations.

The White Revolution

The period 1960–63 marked a turning point in the development of the Iranian state. Industrial expansion was promoted by the Pahlavi regime, while political parties that resisted the shah's absolute consolidation of power were silenced and pushed to the margins. In 1961 the shah dissolved the 20th Majles and cleared the way for the land reform law of 1962. Under this program, the landed minority was forced to give up ownership of vast tracts of land for redistribution to small-scale cultivators. The former landlords were compensated for their loss in the form of shares of state-owned Iranian industries. Cultivators and workers were also given a share in industrial and agricultural profits, and cooperatives began to replace the large landowners in rural areas as sources of capital for irrigation, agrarian maintenance, and development.

The land reforms were a mere prelude to the shah's "White Revolution," a far more ambitious program of social, political, and economic reform. Put to a plebiscite and ratified in 1963, these reforms eventually redistributed land to some 2.5 million families, established literacy and health corps to benefit Iran's rural areas, further reduced the autonomy of tribal groups, and advanced social and legal reforms that furthered the emancipation and enfranchisement of women. In subsequent decades, per capita income for Iranians skyrocketed, and oil revenue fueled an enormous increase in state funding for industrial development projects.

Protest and Failure

The new policies of the shah did not go unopposed, however; many Shīʿite leaders criticized the White Revolution, holding that liberalization laws concerning women were against Islamic values. More important, the shah's reforms chipped away at the traditional bases of clerical power. The development of secular courts had already reduced clerical power over law and jurisprudence, and the reforms' emphasis on secular education further eroded the former monopoly of the ulama in that field. (Paradoxically, the White Revolution's Literacy Corps was to be the only reform implemented by the shah to survive the Islamic revolution, because of its intense popularity.) Most pertinent to clerical independence, land reforms initiated the breakup of huge areas previously held under charitable trust (*vaqf*). These lands were administered by members of the ulama and formed a considerable portion of that class's revenue.

In 1963 a relatively obscure member of the ulama named Ruhollah Musavi Khomeini—a professor of philosophy at the Fayẕiyyeh Madrasah in Qom who was accorded the honorific *ayatollah*—spoke out harshly against the White Revolution's reforms. In response, the government sacked the school, killing several students, and arrested Khomeini. He was later exiled, arriving in Turkey, Iraq, and, eventually, France. During his years of exile, Khomeini stayed in intimate contact with his colleagues in Iran and completed his religio-political doctrine of *velāyat-e faqīh* (Persian: "governance of the jurist"), which provided the theoretical underpinnings for a Shīʿite Islamic state run by the clergy.

Land reform, however, was soon in trouble. The government was unable to put in place a comprehensive support system and infrastructure that replaced the role of the landowner, who had previously provided tenants with all the basic necessities for farming. The result was a high failure rate for new farms and a subsequent flight of agricultural workers and farmers to the country's major cities, particularly Tehrān, where a booming construction industry promised employment. The extended family, the traditional support system in Middle Eastern culture, deteriorated as increasing numbers of young Iranians crowded into the country's largest cities, far from home and in search of work, only to be met by high prices, isolation, and poor living conditions.

Foreign Relations

Domestic reform and industrial development after 1961 were accompanied by an independent national policy in foreign relations, the principles of which were support for the United Nations (UN) and peaceful coexistence with Iran's neighbours. The latter of these principles stressed a positive approach in cementing mutually beneficial ties with other countries. Iran played a major role with Turkey and Pakistan in the Central Treaty Organization (CENTO) and Regional Cooperation for Development (RCD). It also embarked on trade and cultural relations with France, West Germany, Scandinavia, eastern Europe, and the Soviet Union.

Relations with the United States remained close, reflected by the increasing predominance of Western culture in the country and the growing number of American advisers, who were necessary to administer the shah's ambitious economic reforms and, most important, to aid in the development of Iran's military. The Iranian army was the cornerstone of the country's foreign policy and had become, thanks to American aid and expertise, the most powerful, well-equipped force in the region and one of the largest armed forces in the world.

The Growth of Social Discontent

Petroleum revenues continued to fuel Iran's economy in the 1970s, and in 1973 Iran concluded a new 20-year oil agreement with the consortium of Western firms led by British Petroleum. This agreement gave direct control of Iranian oil fields to the government under the auspices of the NIOC and initiated a standard seller-buyer relationship between the NIOC and the oil companies. The shah was acutely aware of the danger of depending on a diminishing oil asset and pursued a policy of economic diversification. Iran had begun automobile production in the 1950s and by the early 1970s was exporting motor vehicles to Egypt and Yugoslavia. The government exploited the country's copper reserves, and in 1972 Iran's first steel mill began producing structural steel. Iran also invested heavily overseas and continued to press for barter agreements for the marketing of its petroleum and natural gas.

This apparent success, however, veiled deep-seated problems. World monetary instability and fluctuations in Western oil consumption seriously threatened an economy that had been rapidly expanding since the early 1950s and that was still directed on a vast scale toward high-cost development programs and large military expenditures. A decade of extraordinary economic growth, heavy government spending, and a boom in oil prices led to high rates of inflation, and—in spite of an elevated level of employment, held artificially high by loans and credits—the buying power of Iranians and their overall standard of living stagnated. Prices skyrocketed as supply failed to keep up with demand, and a 1975 government-sponsored war on high prices resulted in arrests and fines of traders and manufacturers, injuring confidence in the market. The agricultural sector, poorly managed in the years since land reform, continued to decline in productivity.

The shah's reforms also had failed completely to provide any degree of political participation. The sole political outlet within Iran was the rubber-stamp Majles, dominated since the time of Mosaddeq by two parties, both of which were subservient to and sponsored by the shah. Traditional parties such as the National Front had been marginalized, while others, such as the Tūdeh Party, were outlawed and forced to operate covertly. Protest all too often took the form of subversive and violent activity by groups such as the Mojāhedīn-e Khalq and Fedā'īyān-e Khalq, organizations with both Marxist and religious tendencies. All forms of social and political protest, either from the intellectual left or the religious right, were subject to censorship, surveillance, or harassment by SAVAK, and illegal detention and torture were common.

Many argued that since Iran's brief experiment with parliamentary democracy and communist politics had failed, the country had to go back to its indigenous culture. The 1953 coup against Mosaddeq had particularly incensed the intellectuals. For the first time in more than half a century, the secular intellectuals, many of whom were fascinated by the populist appeal of Ayatollah Khomeini, abandoned their project of reducing the authority and power of the Shīʿite ulama and argued that, with the help of the clerics, the shah could be overthrown.

In this environment, members of the National Front, the Tūdeh Party, and their various splinter groups now joined the ulama in a broad opposition to the shah's regime. Khomeini had continued to preach in exile about the evils of the Pahlavi regime, accusing the shah of irreligion and subservience to foreign powers. Thousands of tapes and print copies of the ayatollah's speeches were smuggled back into Iran during the 1970s as an increasing number of unemployed and working-poor Iranians—mostly new immigrants from the countryside, who were disenchanted by the cultural vacuum of modern urban Iran—turned to the ulama for guidance. The shah's dependence on the United States, his close ties with Israel—then engaged in extended hostilities with the overwhelmingly Muslim

Arab states—and his regime's ill-considered economic policies served to fuel the potency of dissident rhetoric with the masses.

THE ISLAMIC REPUBLIC

Outwardly, with a swiftly expanding economy and a rapidly modernizing infrastructure, everything was going well in Iran. But in little more than a generation, Iran had changed from a traditional, conservative, and rural society to one that was industrial, modern, and urban. There was a sense that in both agriculture and industry too much had been attempted too soon and that the government, either through corruption or incompetence, had failed to deliver all that was promised. This discontent was manifested in demonstrations against the regime in 1978 that would swiftly and drastically change the form of Iranian government.

The Islamic Revolution, 1978–79

In January 1978, incensed by what they considered to be slanderous remarks made against Khomeini in a Tehrān newspaper, thousands of young madrasah students took to the streets. They were followed by thousands more Iranian youth—mostly unemployed recent immigrants from the countryside—who began protesting the regime's excesses. The shah, weakened by cancer and stunned by the sudden outpouring of hostility against him, vacillated, assuming the protests to be part of an international conspiracy against him. Many people were killed by government forces in the ensuing chaos, serving only to fuel the violence in a Shīʿite country where martyrdom played a fundamental role in religious expression. In spite of all government efforts, a cycle of violence began in which

Ayatollah Ruhollah Khomeini (left) being greeted by supporters in Tehrān following 15 years in exile. Khomeini was the driving force behind Iran's Islamic Revolution of 1978-79. Gabriel Duval/AFP/Getty Images

each death fueled further protest, and all protest—from the secular left and religious right—became subsumed under the cloak of Shīʿite Islam.

During his exile, Khomeini coordinated this upsurge of opposition—first from Iraq and after 1978 from France—demanding the shah's abdication. In January 1979, in what was officially described as a "vacation," he and his family fled Iran; he died the following year in Cairo.

The Regency Council established to run the country during the shah's absence proved unable to function, and Prime Minister Shahpur Bakhtiar, hastily appointed by the shah before his departure, was incapable of effecting compromise with either his former National Front colleagues or Khomeini. Crowds in excess of a million demonstrated in Tehrān, proving the wide appeal of Khomeini, who arrived in Iran amid wild rejoicing on February 1. Ten days later Bakhtiar went into hiding, eventually to find exile in France, where he was assassinated in 1991.

Postrevolutionary Chaos

On April 1, following overwhelming support in a national referendum, Khomeini declared Iran an Islamic republic. Elements within the clergy promptly moved to exclude their former left-wing, nationalist, and intellectual allies from any positions of power in the new regime, and a return to conservative social values was enforced. The family protection act, which provided further guarantees and rights to women in marriage, was declared void, and mosque-based revolutionary bands known as *komītehs* (Persian: "committees") patrolled the streets enforcing Islamic codes of dress and behaviour and dispatching impromptu justice to perceived enemies of the revolution. Throughout most of 1979 the Revolutionary Guards—then an informal religious militia formed by Khomeini to forestall another CIA-backed coup as in the days of Mosaddeq—engaged in similar activity, aimed at intimidating and repressing political groups not under control of the ruling Revolutionary Council and its sister Islamic Republican Party, both clerical organizations loyal to Khomeini. The violence and brutality often exceeded that of SAVAK under the shah.

The militias and the clerics they supported made every effort to suppress Western cultural influence, and, facing persecution and violence, many of the Western-educated elite fled the country. This

Iran Hostage Crisis

On Nov. 4, 1979, militants in Iran seized 66 American citizens at the U.S. embassy in Tehrān and held 52 of them hostage for more than a year. The hostage crisis, which took place during the chaotic aftermath of Iran's Islamic revolution (1978–79) and its overthrow of the Pahlavi monarchy, had dramatic effects on domestic politics in the United States and on U.S.-Iranian relations for decades.

From the fall of 1978, the U.S. embassy in Tehrān had been the scene of frequent demonstrations by Iranians who opposed the American presence in the country, and on Feb. 14, 1979, the embassy was attacked and briefly occupied. The embassy weathered this assault, but, as a result, the embassy staff was cut, from more than 1,400 before the revolution to about 70 by the start of the hostage crisis.

In October 1979 U.S. authorities informed the Iranian prime minister, Mehdi Bazargan, of Mohammad Reza Shah Pahlavi's impending arrival on American soil for medical treatment. Bazargan, in light of the February attack, guaranteed the safety of the U.S. embassy and its staff. The shah arrived in New York City on October 22, and on November 4 the embassy was attacked by a mob of perhaps 3,000 who, after a short siege, took 63 American men and women hostage. (Three members of the U.S. diplomatic staff were seized at the Iranian Foreign Ministry.) Within the next few days, representatives of U.S. Pres. Jimmy Carter and Tehrān-based diplomats from other countries attempted but failed to free the hostages.

It soon became evident that no one within the anti-American atmosphere of postrevolutionary Iran was willing, or able, to release the hostages. The hostage takers themselves most likely were supporters of revolutionary leader Ayatollah Ruhollah Khomeini—whose failure to order the release of the hostages led Bazargan to resign the premiership on November 6—and demanded, as a condition of the hostages' release, the extradition of the shah to Iran.

In response to the crisis, the United States refused to purchase Iranian oil, froze billions of dollars of Iranian assets in the United States, and engaged in a vigorous campaign of international diplomacy against the Iranians. The consensus of the international community was against the Iranian seizure of the hostages, and diplomats from various countries sought to intervene on their behalf.

One notable incident occurred on Jan. 28, 1980, when Canadian diplomats helped six American diplomats who had managed to avoid capture flee Iran.

By early April 1980 the U.S. administration was seeking a military option. On April 24 a small U.S. task force landed in the desert southeast of Tehrān, intending to stage a quick raid of the embassy compound, convey the hostages to a previously secured airstrip, and then withdraw by air. However, the operation was fraught with problems and, following the malfunction of two of the operation's helicopters, U.S. forces sought to withdraw without completing the mission. One of the remaining helicopters collided with a support aircraft, however, killing eight U.S. service members. All diplomatic initiatives in the hostage crisis came to a standstill, and the hostages were placed, incommunicado, in new, concealed locations.

In spite of the impasse, later events made a resolution of the crisis seem more likely. In mid-August Iran finally installed a new government, and the Carter administration immediately sought to extend diplomatic overtures. Although the start of the Iran-Iraq War (1980–88) temporarily distracted Iranian officials from hostage negotiations, the embargo continued to wear away at the Iranian economy and the country's ability to stave off Iraqi forces. Likewise, when Iranian Prime Minister Mohammad Ali Raja'i visited the UN in October, numerous world leaders made it clear to him that Iran could not expect support in the Iraq conflict as long as it held the U.S. hostages.

As a consequence, Iranian officials engaged in negotiations with renewed vigour. Raja'i insisted against direct negotiations, however, and Algerian diplomats mediated the remainder of the process. Negotiations continued into early 1981, and—an agreement having been made—the hostages were released on Jan. 20, 1981.

anti-Western sentiment eventually manifested itself in the November 1979 seizure of the U.S. embassy by a group of Iranian protesters demanding the extradition of the shah, who at that time was undergoing medical treatment in the United States. Through the embassy takeover, Khomeini's supporters could claim to be as "anti-imperialist" as the political left. This ultimately gave them the ability to suppress most of the regime's left-wing and moderate opponents. The Assembly of Experts (Majles-e Khobregān), overwhelmingly dominated by clergy, ratified a new constitution the following month. Taking 66 U.S. citizens hostage at their embassy proved to highlight the fractures that had begun to occur within the revolutionary regime itself. Moderates, such as provisional Prime Minister Mehdi Bazargan and the republic's first president, Abolhasan Bani-Sadr, who opposed holding the hostages, were steadily forced from power by conservatives within the government who questioned their revolutionary zeal.

The Iran-Iraq War (1980–88)

The new constitution created a religious government based on Khomeini's vision of *velāyat-e faqīh* and gave sweeping powers to the *rahbar*, or leader; the first *rahbar* was Khomeini himself. In spite of the regime's political consolidation, several new threats manifested themselves. The most significant of these was the eight-year period of armed conflict during the Iran-Iraq War.

In September 1980 a long-standing border dispute served as a pretext for Iraqi Pres. Ṣaddām Ḥussein to launch an invasion of Iran's southwestern province of Khūzestān, one of the country's most important oil-producing regions and one populated by many ethnic Arabs. Iran's formidable armed forces had played an important role in ensuring regional stability under the shah but had virtually dissolved after the collapse of the monarch's regime. The weakened military proved to be unexpectedly resilient in the face of the Iraqi assault, however, and, in spite of initial losses, achieved remarkable defensive success.

The Iraqis also provided support to the Mojāhedīn-e Khalq, now headquartered in Iraq. The Mojāhedīn launched a campaign of sporadic and highly demoralizing bombings throughout Iran that killed many clerics and government leaders. In June 1981 a dissident Islamist faction (apparently unrelated to the Mojāhedīn) bombed the headquarters of the Islamic Republican Party, killing a number of leading clerics. Government pressure intensified after the bombing, and Bani-Sadr (who had earlier gone into hiding to avoid arrest) and Massoud Rajavi, the head of the Mojāhedīn, fled the country. The new president, Mohammad Ali Raja'i, and Prime Minister Mohammad Javad Bahonar died in another bombing in August. These attacks led to an unrelenting campaign of repression and executions by the Revolutionary Guards, often based on trivial allegations, to root out subversion. Allegations of torture, poor prison conditions, arbitrary arrests, and the denial of basic human rights proliferated, as did accusations that condemned female prisoners were raped—purportedly forced into temporary marriages (known as *mut'ah*) with their guards before execution.

By the summer of 1982, Iraq's initial territorial gains had been recaptured by Iranian troops who were stiffened with Revolutionary Guards. It also became apparent that young boys, often plucked from the streets, were leading human wave assaults on the front lines, thereby sacrificing their bodies to clear minefields for the troops that followed. These tactics eventually enabled Iran to capture small amounts of Iraqi territory, but the war soon lapsed into stalemate and attrition. In addition, its length caused anxiety among the Arab states and the international community because it posed a potential threat to the oil-producing countries of the Persian Gulf. The civilian populations of both Iran and Iraq suffered severely as military operations moved to bombing population centres and industrial targets, particularly oil refineries. Attacks on oil tankers from both sides greatly curtailed shipping in the gulf.

Finally, in July 1988, after a series of Iraqi offensives during which that country recaptured virtually all of its lost territory, Khomeini announced Iran's acceptance of a UN resolution that required both sides to withdraw to their respective borders and observe a cease-fire, which came into force in August.

The cease-fire redirected attention to long-standing factional conflicts over economic, social, and foreign policy objectives that had arisen between several groups in Iran's government. "Conservatives" favoured less government control of the economy, while "leftists" sought greater economic socialization. These two blocs, both committed to social and religious conservatism, were increasingly challenged by a "pragmatist" or "reformist" bloc. The latter favoured steps to normalize relations with the West, ease strict social restrictions, and open up the country's political system as the only solution to their country's crushing economic and social problems, deeply exacerbated by eight years of war.

Domestic Affairs and Internal Reform

Change began in short order, when the Assembly of Experts appointed Pres. Ali Khamenei *rahbar* following the death of Khomeini in June 1989. The following month elections were held to select Khamenei's replacement as president. Running virtually unopposed, Hojatoleslām Ali Akbar Hashemi Rafsanjani, speaker of the Majles since 1980, was elected by an overwhelming vote. Rafsanjani, whose cabinet choices represented the various factions, immediately began the process of rebuilding the war-torn economy. Considered a pragmatist and one of the most powerful men in Iran, Rafsanjani favoured a policy of economic liberalization, privatization of industry, and rapprochement with the West that would encourage much-needed foreign investment. The new president's policies were opposed by both Khamenei and the conservative parliament, and attempts by conservative elements to stifle reforms by harassing and imprisoning political dissidents frequently resulted in demonstrations and violent protest, which were often brutally suppressed.

In this new political atmosphere, advocates of women's rights joined with filmmakers who continued to address the gender inequities of the Islamic republic. New forms of communication, including satellite dishes and the Internet, created for Iranians access to Western media and exile groups abroad, who, in turn, helped broadcast dissident voices from within Iran. International campaigns for human rights, women's rights, and a nascent democratic civil society in Iran began to take root.

Inside Iran in the mid-1990s, Abdolkarim Soroush, a philosopher with both secular and religious training, attracted thousands of followers to his lectures. Soroush advocated a type of reformist Islam that went beyond most liberal Muslim thinkers of the 20th century and argued that the search for reconciliation of Islam and democracy was not a matter of simply finding appropriate phrases in the Qur'ān that were in agreement with modern science, democracy, or human rights. Drawing on the works of Immanuel Kant, G.W.F. Hegel, Karl Popper, and Erich Fromm, Soroush called for a reexamination of all tenets of Islam, insisting on the need to maintain the religion's original spirit of social justice and its emphasis on caring for other people.

The May 1997 election of Mohammad Khatami, a supporter of Soroush, as president was a surprise for conservatives who had backed Ali Akbar Nateq-Nouri, speaker of Iran's Majles. Shortly before the elections, the Council of Guardians had placed Khatami on a list of four acceptable candidates in order to give a greater semblance of democracy to the process. Khatami had been Iran's minister of culture and Islamic guidance but was forced to resign in 1992 for having adopted a more moderate view on social and cultural issues. He campaigned for president on a platform of curbing censorship, fighting religious excess, and allowing for greater tolerance and was embraced by much of the public, receiving more than two-thirds of the vote and enjoying especially strong support among women and young adults.

The election of Khatami, and his appointment of a more moderate cabinet, unleashed a wave of euphoria among reformers. In less than a year some 900 new newspapers and journals received authorization to publish and added their voices to earlier reformist journals such as *Zanān* and *Kiyān*, which had been the strongest backers of Khatami. However, the limits of the reformist president's authority became clear in the months after his election. The *rahbar*, Ayatollah Khamenei, continued to exercise sweeping executive powers, which he did not hesitate to use to thwart Khatami's reforms. In June 1998 the parliament removed Khatami's liberal interior minister, Abdullah Nouri, in a vote of no confidence, and Tehrān's mayor, Gholamhossein Karbaschi, was convicted of corruption and jailed by the president's conservative opponents in spite of strong public opinion in his favour. Reformist newspapers were accused of offending Islamic principles and shut down one by one, and six prominent intellectuals, including secular nationalist leader Dariyush Farouhar and his wife, Parvaneh Eskandari, were assassinated. Their murders were traced to agents of the Iranian intelligence services, whose representatives claimed that the assassins were acting without orders.

In the February 1999 elections for roughly 200,000 seats on village, town, and city councils, reformers once again won by an overwhelming margin, and many women were elected to office in rural areas. The antidemocratic nature of the office of *rahbar* was vigorously debated, and calls for its removal from the constitution now began to appear in the press. In July 1999 students protested the closing of the *Salām* newspaper and opposed further restrictions on the press; and police, backed by a vigilante group known as Anṣār-e Ḥezbollāh, attacked a dormitory at Tehrān University. Four students were reported killed, and hundreds more were injured or detained. On the day after the attack, 25,000 students staged a sit-in at the university and demanded the resignation of Tehrān's police chief, whom they held responsible for the raid. Within 48 hours, demonstrations had erupted in at least 18 major cities, including Gīlān, Mashhad, and Tabrīz in the north and Yazd, Eṣfahān, and Shīrāz in the south. The demonstrators demanded that the murderers of the Farouhars and other intellectuals be brought to swift justice. They also called for freedom of the press, an increase in personal liberty, an end to the vigilante attacks on universities, and the release of 13 Iranian Jews who had been arrested by the government on allegations that they were spying for Israel. This was the first major student demonstration since the Islamic revolution, and it lasted for five days. By mid-July the government had quelled the protests, and hundreds more were arrested.

In 2001 President Khatami was reelected by an overwhelming majority. Although his victory was considered an expression of support for his programs of reform, at the beginning of his second term there was less popular confidence in his ability to bring about swift and dramatic political change. Attempts by the judiciary to curb pro-reform elements accelerated after Khatami's reelection, including arrests and acts of public censure. In November 2002 Hashem Aghajari, a prominent reform-minded academic, was sentenced to death by a court in western Iran following a speech he made in support of religious reform, sparking the largest student protests since those of 1999. Aghajari's death sentence was subsequently reduced, reinstated, and reduced again before he was released on bail in August 2004.

Mohammad Khatami

(b. Sept. 29, 1943, Ardakān, Iran)

Mohammad Khatami (also spelled Muḥammad Khātamī) is an Iranian political leader who was president of Iran (1997–2005).

The son of a well-known religious teacher, Khatami studied at a traditional madrasah (religious school) in the holy city of Qom, where he later taught. However, he also received degrees in philosophy from Eṣfahān University and the University of Tehrān, both secular institutions, a somewhat unusual accomplishment for a member of Iran's Shīʿite clergy. Khatami held the title *hojatoleslām*, signifying his position as a cleric, and, as a direct descendant of the Prophet Muhammad, he wore a black turban.

During the 1960s and '70s Khatami gained a reputation as an opponent of the rule of Mohammad Reza Shah Pahlavi. In 1978 he was appointed head of the Islamic Centre Hamburg in Germany, and after the revolution he was elected to the Majles, the Iranian national assembly. Khatami held several positions in the Iranian government during the 1980s, including that of minister of culture and Islamic guidance, which he held again in the early 1990s before being forced to resign in 1992 amid allegations that he permitted too much un-Islamic sentiment. He then became the director of the National Library and served as an adviser to Pres. Ali Akbar Hashemi Rafsanjani.

In the 1997 elections Khatami was one of four candidates to run for the presidency and was the most moderate on social issues. With strong support from the country's youth, women, and intellectuals, he was elected by almost 70 percent of the vote. Some of the moderates he appointed to the cabinet were controversial but nonetheless were approved by Iran's conservative Majles. Tension between the president and conservatives grew, however, and, beginning in 1998, a number of key Khatami supporters were prosecuted and harassed as a result. He advocated increased contact with the United States, but his domestic opponents hindered rapprochement between the two countries. Khatami was reelected in 2001 by an overwhelming majority of the vote. Constitutionally barred from a third consecutive term as president, he left office in 2005. In February 2009 he announced his candidacy in the presidential election set for later that year, although he reversed his decision the following month in order to strengthen the chances of Mir Hossein Mousavi, a reformist candidate expected to have a better chance at victory.

Conservatives Return to Power

In the month before the Majles elections scheduled for February 2004, the Council of Guardians announced that almost half the candidates in a pool of some 8,000, including many reformists, would be disqualified from participating in the coming elections. The decision—which entailed a ban on some 80 sitting members of the Majles, including President Khatami's brother—sparked a political crisis, and Khatami himself was among those who subsequently threatened to resign if the ban were not lifted. Following direct intervention by Ayatollah Khamenei, the council reinstated some of the candidates; nevertheless, the conservatives, as expected, emerged victorious in the elections, replacing the more moderate outgoing cabinet.

In January 2005, elections to select Khatami's successor were set for June of that year. In May more than 1,000 presidential candidates were disqualified by the Council of

Guardians from standing in the elections. In the first round of balloting, none of the seven candidates who finally participated surpassed the necessary 50 percent threshold to win outright, and a runoff was held the following week between former president Hashemi Rafsanjani, who had come in first in the initial round, and Mahmoud Ahmadinejad, the conservative mayor of Tehrān who unexpectedly placed a close second. Subsequently, Ahmadinejad defeated Rafsanjani, securing more than 60 percent of the votes cast.

In contrast to his reform-oriented predecessor, Ahmadinejad generally took a more conservative approach domestically—in 2005 he prohibited state television and radio stations from broadcasting music considered "indecent"—though under his leadership women symbolically were allowed for the first time since the revolution into major sporting events. However, Ahmadinejad's failure to satisfactorily address continued high rates of inflation and unemployment during his term led to increasing discontent, damaging his favour among segments of both the populace and the administration. His provocative stance regarding Iran's nuclear program was also a source of criticism among portions of the country's pragmatic conservative leadership. Thus, although conservative elements consolidated their control of the Majles in the elections of March 2008—once more, many reformist candidates were banned—the presence of conservative elements critical of Ahmadinejad's policies prepared the way for greater confrontation between the president and the Majles.

Although no Iranian president had yet failed to win a second term, as the 2009 presidential election approached, some observers believed that Ahmadinejad's economic policies and his confrontational style abroad might have rendered him susceptible to a challenge. Ahmadinejad appeared at particular risk of being unseated by one of his moderate challengers, former prime minister Mir

Hossein Mousavi, around whom much of the country's moderate contingent had coalesced. Voter turnout at the election in mid-June was estimated to reach record highs (polling hours were extended four times to accommodate the turnout), a factor that some interpreted as favourable to Mousavi. Shortly after the polls closed, Mousavi—who claimed he had been contacted by the interior ministry to inform him of his victory—announced that he had won the election outright by a large margin; shortly thereafter, however, officials made a similar announcement in favour of Ahmadinejad. Although Ahmadinejad insisted that the election had been fair and that his mandate had been broadened by the large turnout and the scope of his victory, his opponents alleged electoral fraud. Mousavi urged his supporters to protest the results, and, in the days following the election, massive demonstrations—some of them violent—unfolded in the capital and elsewhere. Although Ayatollah Khamenei initially upheld the election results, he subsequently called for an official inquiry by the Council of Guardians (a body of jurists that reviews legislation and supervises elections) into the allegations of electoral irregularities. The decision was quickly followed by an announcement by the Council of Guardians that the vote would be subject to a partial recount, a motion that fell short of the annulment the opposition had sought.

On June 19, following nearly a week of opposition demonstrations against the election results, Khamenei issued his first public response to the unrest: Before a crowd of supporters at Friday prayers, he again backed Ahmadinejad's victory and warned the opposition against further demonstrations. Subsequent protests were greeted with increasing brutality—various reports indicated that between 10 and 20 protesters had been killed—as well as threats of further confrontation. On June 22 the Council of Guardians confirmed that 50 constituencies had returned more votes than there were registered voters (the opposition alleged that as many as some three times that number of constituencies had a turnout greater than 100 percent of eligible voters). Although irregularities in those 50 constituencies bore the potential to affect some three million votes, the Council of Guardians indicated that this would not change the outcome of the election itself. Following the completion of its partial recount, the council solidified Ahmadinejad's victory by confirming the election results, and in early August Ahmadinejad was sworn in for his second term as president.

Foreign Affairs Since 1989: Continuing Tension Abroad

During his presidency Rafsanjani pushed for restoring economic relations with the West, but Iran, in spite of its long conflict with Iraq, chose not to join the UN multinational force opposing the invasion of Kuwait. In autumn 1991 Iran moved toward reducing its involvement in Lebanon, which facilitated the release of Westerners held hostage there by Lebanese Shīʿite extremists. However, the Iranian government opposed the Israeli-Palestinian peace process and continued to support Islamic groups in Lebanon and in areas under the control of the newly created Palestinian Authority. Iran also allegedly gave financial support to Islamic activists, both Sunni and Shīʿite, in Algeria, The Sudan, Afghanistan, and Tajikistan.

Relations with western Europe and the United States fluctuated. The bounty placed by Iran's government on author Salman Rushdie on charges of blasphemy, as well as the state-supported assassinations of dozens of prominent Iranian dissidents in Europe, prevented Iran from normalizing relations with many western European countries. In 1992 Sadeq Sharafkandi, a prominent member of the Democratic Party of Iranian Kurdistan, and three of his aides were gunned downed in Berlin. The case against those held responsible for the attack was tried in German courts for four years, and in 1997 German authorities indirectly implicated Iranian leaders, including both President Rafsanjani and Ayatollah Khamenei, in the killings. Germany cut off diplomatic and trade relations with Iran, but other European governments continued their economic ties, preventing Iran's complete isolation.

Most Iranian dissident groups in exile gradually shed their divergent views and agreed that they should work for a democratic political order in Iran. One remaining exception was the National Liberation Army of Iran, a leftist Islamic group based in Iraq that was set up by the Mojāhedīn-e Khalq. But change was evident even in this organization; its officer corps had become mostly female, including many educated Iranians from Europe and the United States.

Iranian Pres. Mahmoud Ahmadinejad addresses a crowd gathered in Tehrān in 2010. President Ahmadinejad has been a staunch defender of Iran's nuclear program. Atta Kenare/AFP/Getty Images

Difficult relations between Iran and the United States grew more complex in the wake of the Sept. 11, 2001, attacks on the World Trade Center in New York City. Iranian leadership condemned the attacks, though it also sharply opposed U.S. military intervention in Afghanistan the following month. In January 2002 in his State of the Union address, U.S. Pres. George W. Bush categorized Iran as a member of the "axis of evil" (with the regimes of Iraq and North Korea, whom he also described as seeking weapons of mass destruction), an association that was immediately condemned in Iran. U.S. plans for a military intervention in Iraq, a move criticized by Pres. Khatami for its potential to increase instability in the region, also strained the relationship.

Among the most contentious of Iran's foreign policy issues at the beginning of the 21st century was the ongoing question of the development of its nuclear capabilities. Iran insisted that its nuclear pursuits were intended for peaceful purposes, but the international community, expressing deep suspicion that Iran's activities included the development of nuclear weapons, advocated efforts to suspend them. The nuclear issue remained at the forefront during the tenure of President Ahmadinejad, a staunch defendant of Iran's program who indicated the country's intent to continue its nuclear activities in spite of both incentive packages and sanctions put forth by the international community. A National Intelligence Estimate (NIE) report issued by the U.S. intelligence community in December 2007 indicated with high confidence that Iran had halted its nuclear weapons program in 2003 and assessed with moderate confidence that work had not resumed by mid-2007; however, in February 2008 the International Atomic Energy Agency suggested that there existed evidence that Iran had in fact continued nuclear development after the 2003 date put forth by the NIE.

CONCLUSION

The heart of the storied Persian empire of antiquity, Iran has long played an important role in the region as an imperial power and later—because of its strategic position and abundant natural resources, especially petroleum—as a factor in colonial and superpower rivalries. From its roots as a distinctive society about 550 BCE, the region that is now Iran—traditionally known as Persia—has been influenced by waves of indigenous and foreign conquerors and immigrants, including the Seleucids, Parthians, and Sāsānids. It was Persia's conquest by the Muslim Arabs in the 7th century CE, however, that was to leave the most lasting influence.

Rather than entirely overwhelming Iran's pre-Islamic cultural heritage, Arab conquest complemented it, bringing fresh religious and linguistic endowments and contributing to a revitalized cultural amalgam. Shīʿite Islam in particular found firm ground and would thereafter come to exert a powerful influence on Iranian cultural identity. In the 16th century Twelver Shīʿism was enshrined as the state religion under the Ṣafavids, laying the foundation for modern Iran as one of only a handful of Islamic republics and as the world's only Shīʿite state. Likewise, the Arabization of the Persian language—marked by the use of the Arabic script, the medium of the Qur'ān—and the adoption of a broad tableau of Arabic terms may also be traced to the Arab, Muslim culture that spurred it and the Persian cultural renaissance that followed the conquest.

Claimed over subsequent centuries by diverse dynasties of local and foreign origin in turn, Iran was greeted in the modern period by European colonialist competition in pursuit of the country's strategic benefits. With the growth of European involvement in Iranian affairs, however, difficult questions about Western influence, the scope of reform, and political identity were raised. Cultural, political, and socioeconomic concerns—and conflict between those who sought reforms and those who were opposed to (or disappointed by) them—coalesced to find a powerful popular voice at the end of the 1970s. Iran's Islamic revolution succeeded in drastically changing the face of Iranian government to a unique combination of parliamentary democracy and theocracy. Although the Islamic republic established in the 1970s remains in place in the early 21st century, in many ways the tension between conservative and moderate, or reformist, elements—and the wide range of questions it has raised—continues in Iran today.

GLOSSARY

ayatollah A high-ranking religious authority in the Shīʿite branch of Islam, regarded by his followers as the most learned person of his age.

caliph A successor of Muhammad as temporal and spiritual head of Islam.

dry farming The cultivation of crops without irrigation in regions of limited moisture.

Farsi The Iranian language spoken by more than 25 million people in Iran as a first language, and by millions more as a second.

Hadith Indo-Islamic tradition, or collection of traditions, attributed to the Prophet Muhammad that include his sayings, acts, and approval or disapproval of things.

imam The head of the Muslim community.

kavīrs The salt flats of Iran, produced when areas of accumulated water evaporate.

kharāj A special tax that was demanded from recent converts to Islam during the 7th and 8th centuries.

madrasah Islamic theological seminary and law school attached to a mosque.

mahdi In Islamic eschatology, a messianic deliverer who will fill the Earth with justice and equity, restore true religion, and usher in a short golden age before the end of the world.

Majles Iran's unicameral legislature; also known as the Islamic Consultative Assembly.

mujtahid One who is empowered to interpret legal issues not explicitly addressed in the Qur'ān.

mullah An educated Muslim trained in traditional religious law and doctrine.

Nestorian Member of a Christian sect that originated in Asia Minor and Syria holding that Christ had separate divine and human natures.

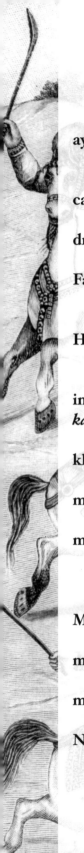

qanāt An ancient, underground system of trenches and wells that delivered water to arid regions.

sayyids Member of the family of Muhammad who are not his direct descendents through the line of the 12th imam.

Semite A person who speaks one of a group of related languages, presumably derived from a common language. The term came to include Arabs, Akkadians, Canaanites, some Ethiopians, and Aramaean tribes, including Hebrews.

ulama Community of scholars made up of male Muslims who have attended a madrasah.

xenophobia Fear or hatred of strangers or foreigners or of anything strange or foreign.

zakāt An obligatory alms tax levied on Muslims, one of the five Pillars of Islam.

Zoroastrianism Ancient religion that originated in Iran based on the teachings of Zoroaster, an early religious reformer and prophet.

BIBLIOGRAPHY

GEOGRAPHY

W.B. Fisher (ed.), *The Land of Iran* (1968), vol. 1 of *The Cambridge History of Iran*, is among the most comprehensive works on geography and social ecology. Jamshid A. Momeni (ed.), *The Population of Iran: A Selection of Readings* (1977), covers all aspects of Iran's human resources. Studies of various peoples include Fredrik Barth, *Nomads of South-Persia: The Basseri Tribe of the Khamseh Confederacy* (1961, reissued 1986); and Lois Beck, *The Qashqa'i of Iran* (1986), a political ethnography. The essays in Richard Tapper (ed.), *The Conflict of Tribe and State in Iran and Afghanistan* (1983), assess tribal political and social structures.

Charles Issawi (ed.), *The Economic History of Iran, 1800–1914* (1971), contains useful information on pre-World War I economic conditions. The petroleum and natural gas industries are discussed in Fereidun Fesharaki, *Development of the Iranian Oil Industry: International and Domestic Aspects* (1976). Agrarian reforms and their impact are detailed in Ann K.S. Lambton, *Landlord and Peasant in Persia* (1953, reissued 1991); and Afsaneh Najmabadi, *Land Reform and Social Change in Iran* (1987). On Iran's economy since the Islamic revolution, see Saeed Rahnema and Sohrab Behdad (eds.), *Iran After the Revolution: Crisis of an Islamic State* (1995).

The interconnections of religion and politics are analyzed by Nikki R. Keddie (ed.), *Religion and Politics in Iran: Shi'ism from Quietism to Revolution* (1983). 'Allamah Sayyid Muhammad Husayn Tabataba'i, *Shi'ite Islam*, trans. from Persian by Seyyed Hossein Nasr (1977), studies the origins and growth of Shīʿism. Works on the religious background of the Islamic revolution of 1978–79 include Michael M.J. Fisher, *Iran: From Religious Dispute to Revolution* (1980; reprinted 1982). Human rights in Iran are discussed in

Reza Afshari, *Human Rights in Iran: The Abuse of Cultural Relativism* (2001).

R.W. Ferrier (ed.), *The Arts of Persia* (1989), is an extensive survey that concentrates on Islamic arts. On the Iranian cinema at home and abroad, see Hamid Naficy, *The Making of Exile Cultures: Iranian Television in Los Angeles* (1993).

History

Iran from 640 to c. 1500

An essential reference work is *The Encyclopaedia of Islam*, 4 vol. and supplement (1913–38); a new ed. is in progress (1960–). Iran under Arab governors in the 7th–9th centuries is explored in Richard N. Frye, *The Golden Age of Persia: The Arabs in the East* (1975; reprinted 1996). M.A. Shaban, *The 'Abbāsid Revolution* (1970; reissued 1979), concentrates on the Arab conquest and settlement of Khorāsān. The Ghaznavids are discussed in Clifford Edmund Bosworth, *The Ghaznavids: Their Empire in Afghanistan and Eastern Iran, 994–1040*, 2nd ed. (1973; reissued 1992). Roy P. Mottahedeh, *Loyalty and Leadership in an Early Islamic Society* (1980), focuses on the Būyids. The Seljuqs and Mongols are the subjects of Ann K.S. Lambton, *Continuity and Change in Medieval Persia: Aspects of Administrative, Economic, and Social History, 11th–14th Century* (1988); and David Morgan, *Medieval Persia, 1040–1797* (1988), which covers events up to the Qājār period.

Iran from c. 1500 to c. 1950

Charles Melville (ed.), *Safavid Persia: The History of and Politics of an Islamic Society* (1996), explores many Ṣafavid-era issues. The Qājār period is discussed in Clifford Edmund Bosworth and Carole Hillenbrand (eds.), *Qajar Iran: Political, Social, and Cultural Change, 1800–1925* (1983; reissued

1992). Hamid Algar, *Religion and State in Iran, 1785–1906: The Role of the Ulama in the Qajar Period* (1969, reissued 1980); and Mangol Bayat, *Mysticism and Dissent: Socioreligious Thought in Qajar Iran* (1982), discuss 19th-century religious development. Works on the Constitutional Revolution include Janet Afary, *The Iranian Constitutional Revolution, 1906–1911: Grassroots Democracy, Social Democracy & the Origins of Feminism* (1996); and Vanessa Martin, *Islam and Modernism: The Iranian Revolution of 1906* (1989). Works on the Pahlavi period include Ervand Abrahamian, *Iran Between Two Revolutions* (1982), covering 1905 to 1979; and Fakhreddin Azimi, *Iran: The Crisis of Democracy* (1989).

IRAN SINCE *C.* 1950

The political and socioeconomic background of the Islamic revolution is explored by Nikki R. Keddie and Yann Richard, *Roots of Revolution: An Interpretive History of Modern Iran* (1981); Mohammed Amjad, *Iran: From Royal Dictatorship to Theocracy* (1989); and Misagh Parsa, *Social Origins of the Iranian Revolution* (1989). The religious background of the revolution is covered in Roy Mottahedeh, *The Mantle of the Prophet: Religion and Politics in Iran* (1985, reissued 1987). The Islamic republic itself is the subject of Shaul Bakhash, *The Reign of the Ayatollahs: Iran and the Islamic Revolution*, rev. ed. (1990); Robin Wright, *Sacred Rage: The Crusade of Modern Islam* (1985), and *In the Name of God: The Khomeini Decade* (1989, reissued 1991), which recount Iran's efforts to export its revolution to other Islamic countries. The Iran-Iraq War is analyzed by several pre-armistice works, such as Shahram Chubin and Charles Tripp, *Iran and Iraq at War* (1988, reissued 1991); Majid Khadduri, *The Gulf War: The Origins and Implications of the Iraq-Iran Conflict* (1988); and by several post-armistice publications, including Hanns W. Maull and Otto Pick (eds.), *The Gulf War: Regional and International Dimensions* (1989).

INDEX

A

B

C

S

T

U

V

W

Y

Z